Cuddly Crochet Pets

30 Easy Plushie Patterns to Create Adorable Cats, Dogs & More

Glory Shofowora

Creator of Crafting in Glory and
Author of *Cuddly Crochet Plushies*

PAGE STREET
PUBLISHING CO.

First published in 2026 by
Page Street Publishing Co.
27 Congress Street, Suite 1511
Salem, MA 01970
www.pagestreetpublishing.com

Distributed by Macmillan, sales in Canada by The Canadian Manda Group.

30 29 28 27 26 1 2 3 4 5

ISBN-13: 979-8-89003-449-6

Library of Congress Control Number: 2025948481

Edited by Sarah Monroe
Cover and book design by Molly Kate Young for Page Street Publishing Co.
Photography by Juliana Buenrostro, step-by-step photography by Glory Shofowora

Printed and bound in China

Page Street Publishing protects our planet by donating to nonprofits like The Trustees, which focuses on local land conservation.

To my mother and father,

who continue to show their love and support

for all of my goals

Contents

Introduction

When I learned how to crochet, I had the privilege of learning from my mother. At the time, I was 10 years old—but a decade later, I've continued to crochet. Although I was taught how to crochet practical items like scarves, blankets, and pillows, my mother didn't know the first thing when it came to crocheting stuffed animals. So for that task, I had to learn on my own.

I was able to learn the basics through the internet, but I wasn't able to buy patterns—because I didn't have access to a credit card. This restriction led me to create my own patterns. I would challenge my skills and channel my creativity by crocheting my friends' favorite animals—some of my first projects were their pets. Although I never had a pet of my own, I would interact with stray cats that roamed the streets near my neighborhood or my friends' dogs that were friendly enough to greet me at the door. By my senior year of high school, I had started to share my original patterns on the internet with the world.

As I gained more experience, I started crocheting custom orders for people upon request. Many times, I would make a custom pet for someone and share the picture online, and there would be another person asking for a pattern to make their own. At the time, I never thought of writing down the patterns for the many dogs and cats I created. However, as I made more calicos, blue heelers, and poodles, I had more crocheters asking for patterns.

And that brings us to this book, where I have compiled a collection of 30 pet patterns that I know you will find adorable. Whether you're crocheting your own pet or a friend's pet—or maybe you just really like parrots!—this book has the pattern for you.

So grab a hook, yarn, and stuffing—you're gonna need them!

Yarn & Hook to Use

Throughout this book, you'll notice that I use the same type of yarn and hook for each pattern: #6 super bulky chenille yarn by the brand Premier® Yarns Parfait® Chunky yarn (100% polyester) and a US size H-8 (5mm) hook.

I use a variety of colors for the eyes and noses in my plushies, but you are encouraged to use whichever colors you like. My favorite colors from Premier Yarns Parfait Chunky are: Black, Cocoa, Chocolate, Gray, Key Lime, and Bubblegum.

Although this yarn makes the softest plushies, it isn't always available or desirable for each person. Luckily, all my patterns are designed in a way that even if you crochet using acrylic yarn, you will be able to have the same plushies at home!

Of course, the thicker and bigger your hook, the bigger your plushie will be, and vice versa, so keep that in mind when choosing the yarn you'd like to use for your plushie.

How to Make the Loop Stitch

This stitch is used in many of the patterns to give the effect of extra-fluffy fur!

Place your hook into the next st, yarn over, and draw through a loop. Remove the loop from your hook (image 1), place your hook into the front loop of the same st (image 2), yarn over (image 3), and draw through a loop. Yarn over (image 4) and pull through the remaining 2 sts on your hook (image 5).

2

3

4

5

1

2

How to Crochet Limbs to a Body

Before you start on the patterns, read this part! Almost every plushie in this book utilizes this technique in one way or the other.

When you work on a pattern, the round (Rnd) will say to "attach limb with x sts." In order to attach the limb properly to the body, place your hook into the x st of the limb (image 1). For example, if the pattern says to attach the limb with 5 sts, place your hook into the 5th st of the last Rnd of the limb. When you're placing your hook into the st of the limb, make sure that your hook is going from the wrong side of the piece, through the stitch, and out the right side of the piece.

Then, place your hook into the next st of the body (image 2).

At this stage, it's important that the wrong side (inside) of the body is facing the sky, and the right side (outside) of the limb is seen, so that it will not be inside out (image 3).

Yarn over and draw a loop through both sts. Then, yarn over and draw through both loops (image 4). Essentially, we're single crocheting (sc) the limb to the body.

Repeat this for the remaining sts that the pattern specifies (image 5). To continue the beginning example, you would place your hook into the 4th st of the last Rnd of the limb and the next st of the body and single crochet them together.

Then, place your hook into the 3rd st of the last Rnd of the limb and the next st of the body and single crochet them together. Place your hook into the 2nd st of the last Rnd of the limb and the next st of the body and sc them together. Finally, place your hook into the 1st st of the last Rnd of the limb and the next st of the body and sc them together.

(continued)

Then, sc into the next sts of the body only, and continue to attach each limb the same way we did the first.

Now you've got all your limbs attached to the body—and you didn't have to sew a thing! Now, we can move on to the next Rnd.

The next Rnd will state to "sc in the remaining y sts of the limb." For a better visual, simply crochet in each of the stitches we didn't crochet in the previous round (images 6–7). To continue the previous example, if our limb had 16 sts total and we connected the limb to the body with 5 sts, we will crochet in the 11 sts left untouched. If you don't, you will end up with a hole—and we don't want that. Then, sc in the next sts of the body as stated (image 8).

How to Embroider Eyes to a Face

With each of my plushies, you'll notice that I did not use safety eyes. That's because I embroider each and every eye onto all of them! Although this has its pros and cons, one huge pro is that the plushies made with embroidered eyes are safe for children. So if you're planning to make a plushie for a child, this section is for you.

Using the color you desire, cut a 12-inch (30.5-cm) strand of yarn, and put it through the eye of a tapestry needle. Poke your needle under the st you want to embroider the eye on and through the top of the same st (image 1). Pull the thread through (but not all of it so you can sew the end into the piece later). Poke your needle through the same hole as before, layering your yarn on the left and on the right with every stitch (image 2). Continue to do this until you end up with a circle (image 3). This is the eyeball.

(continued)

For the "sparkle" of the eye, cut a 12-inch (30.5-cm) strand of white yarn and put it through the eye of a tapestry needle. Poke your needle through the eyeball at the top right corner (image 4). Then, bring your needle down along the eye and poke it through a hole one stitch down (image 5). Pull the yarn but not too tightly; you can place another needle in between the st to keep yourself from pulling the yarn too tight (image 6). Sew in the remaining ends.

This technique can be used with any yarn! Some yarn will take more stitches, and some will require fewer. Although this technique takes some practice, it's worth it if you'd like a different feel to your stuffed animals!

I have also included instructions in the patterns for placing safety eyes, if you prefer to use those.

How to Embroider a Classic Nose

Many of my patterns use this simple technique for embroidering a cute triangle nose.

Using the color you desire, cut a 12-inch (30.5-cm) strand of yarn, and put it through the eye of a tapestry needle. Poke your needle in Rnd 3 so that it comes out at the top left (image 1). Count 3 stitches to the right and poke your needle so it goes from the top right back to the bottom of the triangle to form the top of the nose (image 2).

Poke your needle into the same stitch at the top right and again back to the bottom to form the side of the nose (image 3). Do the same on the left, and then fill in the middle the same way (image 4). If you'd like, you can make the nose wider or narrower to suit the shape of your plushie. Weave in both ends.

The Dashing Dogs

Who doesn't love dogs? Dogs are a human's best friend, with over 300 breeds to show for it! Although I included only a small handful of the most popular breeds, feel free to mix and match the patterns to custom fit your dog. After all, your dog, or your loved one's dog, isn't just an animal—it's family—and being able to bring your furry family member to life through yarn is amazing! So grab your yarn, a hook, some polyester fiberfill, and a few pictures of the dog to start on these patterns.

Fiona the French Bulldog

Bulldogs may have a bad rep for being scary, but they're actually one of the sweetest breeds! This pattern allows you to make a simplified version of a complex-looking bulldog—but not so simple that it takes away from its unique look!

Skill Level

Intermediate

Size

Approx 6 inches (15 cm) long, 7 inches (18 cm) wide, and 10 inches (25.5 cm) tall

Yarn

Super chunky chenille yarn, Premier Yarns Parfait Chunky, 100% polyester, 131 yards (120 m), 3.5 oz (100 g)

- Seal (MC), 393 yds (360 m)
- Cream (C1), 131 yds (120 m)

Hooks

US size H-8 (5mm)

Notions

Polyester fiberfill

Removable stitch marker used to mark the first stitch of the round (and other indicated stitches within a round)

Tapestry needle

Pair of 6-mm safety eyes (optional)

Gauge

20 sc x 18 rounds = 4 inches (10 cm)

Abbreviations

C1 = color 1

Ch(s) = chain(s)

Dec = decrease (crochet 2 sc together)

Flo = front loop only

Inc = increase (work 2 sc into one stitch)

MC = main color

MR = magic ring

Sc = single crochet

Sl st = slip stitch

St(s) = stitch(es)

Fiona the French Bulldog Pattern

Legs (make 4)

With MC, make a MR, then sc 8 into the MR (8 sts).

Rnd 1: Inc in each st (16 sts).

Rnds 2–3 (2 Rnds): Sc in each st (16 sts).

Rnd 4: Sc 4, dec 6 times (10 sts).

Rnds 5–9 (5 Rnds): Sc in each st (10 sts).

Sl st into the 1st st of Rnd 9.

Fasten off and leave a 3-inch (7.5-cm) tail. Set aside.

Tail

With MC, make a MR, then sc 8 into the MR (8 sts).

Rnds 1–10 (10 Rnds): Sc in each st (8 sts).

Fasten off and leave a 12-inch (30.5-cm) tail for sewing.

Body

With C1, ch 16. Inc in the 2nd chain from hook, sc in the next 13 chs, inc 2 times in the last ch. Turn your work clockwise 180 degrees, so that you can work along the opposite side of the chain. Then, sc in the next 13 chs, and inc in the last ch (34 sts).

Rnd 1: Inc in the next 2 sts, sc 13, inc in the next 4 sts, sc 13, inc in the last 2 sts (42 sts).

Rnd 2: Sc 2. Attach a Leg by placing your hook into the 8th st of the Leg and the next st of the Body. Sc the sts together. Sc the 7th st of the Leg and the next st of the Body together. Sc the 6th st of the Leg and the next st of the Body together. Sc 12. Attach a Leg in the next 3 sts, the same way that the first Leg was attached. Sc 3. Attach the third Leg by placing your hook into the 10th st of the Leg and the next st of the Body. Sc the sts together. Sc the 1st st of the Leg and the next st of the Body together. Sc the 9th st of the Leg and the next st of the Body together. Sc 12. Attach the last Leg the same way the previous Leg was attached. Sc 1 (42 sts).

Rnd 3: With C1, sc into the first 2 sts of the Body. With MC, sc into the remaining 7 sts of Leg 1. Sc into the next 12 sts of the Body. Sc into the remaining 7 sts of Leg 2. Sc into the next 3 sts of the Body. Sc into the remaining 7 sts of Leg 3. Sc into the next 12 sts of the Body. Sc into the remaining 7 sts of Leg 4. With C1, sc into the remaining st of the Body (58 sts).

Rnds 4–5 (2 Rnds): With C1, sc 3. With MC, sc 54. With C1, sc 1 (58 sts).

Rnds 6–7 (2 Rnds): With C1, sc 4. With MC, sc 53. With C1, sc 1 (58 sts).

Rnd 8: With C1, sc 5. With MC, sc 52. With C1, sc 1 (58 sts). Stuff the Legs.

Rnds 9–11 (3 Rnds): With C1, sc 6. With MC, sc 52 (58 sts).

Rnds 12–13 (2 Rnds): With MC, sc 1. With C1, sc 6. With MC, sc 51 (58 sts).

Rnd 14: With MC, sc 2. With C1, sc 6. With MC, sc 50 (58 sts).

Rnd 15: With MC, sc 2. With C1, sc 6. With MC, sc 12, (dec, sc 3) 6 times, sc 8 (52 sts).

Rnd 16: With MC, sc 3. With C1, sc 6. With MC, sc 43 (52 sts). Stuff the Body.

Rnd 17: With MC, sc 3. With C1, sc 6. With MC, sc 11, (dec, sc 2) 6 times, sc 8 (46 sts).

Rnd 18: With MC, sc 4. With C1, sc 6. With MC, sc 29. Place a st marker in the 22nd st. Place your hook into the next st of the Body and the st marker st. Sl st the sts together. Repeat this process with the next st of the Body and the 21st st, the next st of the Body and the 20th st, the next st of the Body and the 19th st, the next st of the Body and the 18th st, and the next st of the Body and the 17th st. (You will now have 12 sts connected in the middle of the Body, and 2 openings, with 17 sts each.) With C1, sc into the last st of the Body (40 sts). Break MC. Remove the st marker. For more info on this section, refer to Blake the Boxer on page 49.

Rnd 19: With MC, sc 4. With C1, sc 6. With MC, sc 6. Place your hook into the last st of the Rnd, and sc into the st (17 sts).

Rnd 20: With MC, sc 4. With C1, sc 6. With MC, sc 7 (17 sts).

Fasten off and leave a 12-inch (30.5-cm) tail for sewing.

To finish the Body, with MC, place your hook into the 23rd st of Rnd 18. Sc into the same st. With MC, work into the remaining 16 sts by dec 8 times (9 sts).

Rnd 21: (Dec, sc) 3 times (6 sts).

Fasten off and sew the hole closed.

Head

With MC, make a MR, then sc 8 into the MR (8 sts).

Rnd 1: Sc 3 into the 1st st, sc 2, inc in the next st, sc 2, sc 3 into the next st, sc 1 (13 sts).

Rnd 2: Sc, sc 3 into the next st, sc 3, inc in the next 2 sts, sc 3, sc 3 into the next st, sc 2 (19 sts).

Rnds 3–4 (2 Rnds): Sc in each st (19 sts).

Rnd 5: Sc 7. Inc in the flo in the next 5 sts. Sc 7 (24 sts).

Rnd 6: Sc 8, (inc, sc) 4 times, sc 8 (28 sts).

Rnd 7: Sc 6, (inc, sc 3) 4 times, sc 6 (32 sts). Attach safety eyes on this Rnd, 8 sts apart.

Rnds 8–15 (8 Rnds): Sc in each st (32 sts).

Rnd 16: (Dec, sc 2) 8 times (24 sts). Stuff the Head.

Rnd 17: Sc in each st (24 sts).

Rnd 18: (Dec, sc 2) 6 times (18 sts).

Rnd 19: (Dec, sc) 6 times (12 sts).

Rnd 20: Dec 6 times (6 sts).

Fasten off and sew the hole closed.

Ears (make 2)

With MC, make a MR, then sc 6 into the MR (6 sts).

Rnd 1: Sc in each st (6 sts).

Rnd 2: (Inc, sc 2) 2 times (8 sts).

Rnd 3: Sc in each st (8 sts).

Rnd 4: (Inc, sc 3) 2 times (10 sts).

Rnd 5: (Inc, sc 4) 2 times (12 sts).

Rnd 6: (Inc, sc 2) 4 times (16 sts).

Rnds 7–10 (4 Rnds): Sc in each st (16 sts).

Fasten off and leave a 12-inch (30.5-cm) tail for sewing.

Assembly

Sew each Ear onto Rnd 12 of the Head, 4 sts apart. For each Ear, sew Rnd 1 to Rnd 6, creating a bend. Sew the Tail on the back of Rnd 20 of the Body. Sew the Head onto the neck of the Body. If you aren't using safety eyes, embroider a pair of eyes onto Rnd 7 of the Head, 8 sts apart. Finally, embroider a triangle-shaped nose 2 Rnds tall and 3 sts wide at its widest point on the Head.

Callen the Corgi

Corgis are notorious for their small body shape—in fact, the name originates from the Welsh language and means dwarf dog! So, grab your hook and get ready to work on this cutie with tiny legs and a big belly.

Skill Level

Intermediate

Size

Approx 6 inches (15 cm) long, 7 inches (18 cm) wide, and 10 inches (25.5 cm) tall

Yarn

Super chunky chenille yarn, Premier Yarns Parfait Chunky, 100% polyester, 131 yards (120 m), 3.5 oz (100 g)

- Mustard (MC), 393 yds (360 m)
- Cream (C1), 131 yds (120 m)

Hooks

US size H-8 (5mm)

Notions

Polyester fiberfill

Removable stitch marker used to mark the first stitch of the round (and other indicated stitches within a round)

Tapestry needle

Pair of 6-mm safety eyes (optional)

Gauge

20 sc x 18 rounds = 4 inches (10 cm)

Abbreviations

C1 = color 1

Ch(s) = chain(s)

Dec = decrease (crochet 2 sc together)

Flo = front loop only

Inc = increase (work 2 sc into one stitch)

MC = main color

MR = magic ring

Sc = single crochet

Sl st = slip stitch

St(s) = stitch(es)

Callen the Corgi Pattern

Legs (make 4)

With C1, make a MR, then sc 8 into the MR (8 sts).

Rnd 1: Inc in each st (16 sts).

Rnds 2–3 (2 Rnds): Sc in each st (16 sts).

Rnd 4: Sc 4, dec 6 times (10 sts).

Rnds 5–7 (3 Rnds): Sc in each st (10 sts).

Sl st into the 1st st of Rnd 7.

Fasten off and leave a 3-inch (7.5-cm) tail. Set aside.

Tail

With MC, make a MR, then sc 8 into the MR (8 sts).

Rnds 1–4 (4 Rnds): Sc in each st (8 sts).

Fasten off and leave a 12-inch (30.5-cm) tail for sewing.

Body

With C1, ch 16.

Inc in the 2nd chain from hook, sc in the next 13 chs, and inc 2 times in the last ch. Turn your work clockwise 180 degrees, so that you can work along the opposite side of the chain. Then, sc in the next 13 chs, and inc in the last ch (34 sts).

Rnd 1: Inc in the first 2 sts, sc 13, inc in the next 4 sts, sc 13, inc in the last 2 sts (42 sts).

Rnd 2: Sc 2. Attach Leg 1 by placing your hook into the 6th st of the Leg and the next st of the Body. Sc the sts together. Sc the 5th st of the Leg and the next st of the Body. Sc the 4th st of the Leg and the next st of the Body together. Sc 12. Attach Leg 2 the same way the first Leg was attached. Sc 3. Attach the third Leg by placing your hook into the 1st st of the Leg and the next st of the Body. Sc the sts together. Sc the 10th st of the Leg and the next st of the Body together. Sc the 9th st of the Leg and the next st of the Body together. Sc 12. Attach the last Leg the same way the previous Leg was attached. Sc in the last st (42 sts).

Rnd 3: Sc 2. Sc into the remaining 7 sts of Leg 1. Sc into the next 12 sts of the Body. Sc into the remaining 7 sts of Leg 2. Sc into the next 3 sts of the Body.

(Rnd 3 continued)

Sc into the remaining 7 sts of Leg 3. Sc into the next 12 sts of the Body. Sc into the remaining 7 sts of Leg 4. Sc into the remaining st of the Body (58 sts).

Rnd 4: With C1, sc 11. With MC, sc 38. With C1, sc 9 (58 sts).

Rnd 5: With C1, sc 12. With MC, sc 37. With C1, sc 9 (58 sts).

Rnd 6: With C1, sc 12. With MC, sc 38. With C1, sc 8 (58 sts).

Rnd 7: With C1, sc 10. With MC, sc 42. With C1, sc 6 (58 sts).

Rnd 8: With C1, sc 11. With MC, sc 41. With C1, sc 6 (58 sts).

Rnd 9: With C1, sc 11. With MC, sc 42. With C1, sc 5 (58 sts).

Rnd 10: With C1, sc 12. With MC, sc 41. With C1, sc 5 (58 sts).

Rnd 11: With C1, sc 12. With MC, sc 42. With C1, sc 4 (58 sts).

Rnd 12: With C1, sc 13. With MC, sc 41. With C1, sc 4 (58 sts).

Rnd 13: With C1, sc 13. With MC, sc 42. With C1, sc 3 (58 sts).

Rnd 14: With C1, sc 14. With MC, sc 41. With C1, sc 3 (58 sts).

Rnd 15: With C1, sc 14. With MC, sc 6, (dec, sc 3) 6 times, sc 6. With C1, sc 2 (52 sts). Stuff the Legs.

Rnd 16: With C1, sc 15. With MC, sc 35. With C1, sc 2 (52 sts). Start to stuff the Body.

Rnd 17: With C1, sc 15. With MC, sc 5, (dec, sc 2) 6 times, sc 7. With C1, sc in the last st (46 sts).

Rnd 18: With C1, sc 16. With MC, sc 23. Place a st marker in the 22nd st from the beginning of the round. Place your hook into the next st of the Body and the st marker st. Sl st the sts together. Repeat this process with the next st of the Body and the 21st st, the next st of the Body and the 20th st, the next st of the Body and the 19th st, the next st of the Body and the 18th st, and the next st of the Body and the 17th st. (You will now have 12 sts connected in the middle of the Body, and 2 openings, with 17 sts each.) With C1, sc into the last st of the Body (40 sts). Break MC. Remove the st marker. For more info on this section, refer to Blake the Boxer on page 49.

Rnd 19: With C1, sc 16. Sc in the last st (17 sts).

Rnd 20: Sc in each st (17 sts).

Fasten off and leave a 12-inch (30.5-cm) tail for sewing.

To finish the Body, with MC, place your hook into the 23rd st of Rnd 18. Sc into the same st. Work into the remaining 16 sts by dec 8 times (9 sts). Finish stuffing the Body.

Rnd 21: (Dec, sc) 3 times (6 sts).

Fasten off and sew the hole closed.

Head

With C1, make a MR, then sc 8 into the MR (8 sts).

Rnd 1: Inc in each st (16 sts).

Rnds 2–4 (3 Rnds): Sc in each st (16 sts).

Rnd 5: With C1, sc 7. With MC, inc 3 times in the flo. With C1, sc. With MC, inc 3 times. With C1, sc in the last 2 sts (22 sts).

Rnd 6: With C1, sc 7. With MC, (inc, sc) 3 times. With C1, sc 2. With MC, (inc, sc) 3 times. With C1, sc in last st (28 sts). If using, attach safety eyes on this Rnd, 7 sts apart.

Rnd 7: With C1, sc 7. With MC, sc 10. With C1, sc. With MC, sc 9. With C1, sc in last st (28 sts).

Rnd 8: With C1, sc 7. Inc in next st. With MC, (sc 2, inc) 2 times, sc 3. With C1, sc 1. With MC, (inc, sc 2) 3 times. With C1, sc in last st (34 sts).

Rnd 9: With C1, sc 9. With MC, sc 12. With C1, sc. With MC, sc 12 (34 sts).

Rnd 10: With C1, sc 10. With MC, sc 11. With C1, sc. With MC, sc 12 (34 sts).

Rnd 11: With C1, sc 10. With MC, sc 24 (34 sts). Break C1.

Rnd 12: With MC, sc in each st (34 sts).

Rnd 13: Sc 9, (dec, sc 2) 3 times, sc 5, (dec, sc 2) 2 times (29 sts).

Rnd 14: Dec, sc 27 (28 sts).

Rnd 15: Sc in each st (28 sts).

Rnd 16: Sc 11, (dec, sc) 5 times, dec (22 sts).

Rnd 17: (Dec, sc 3, dec, sc 4) 2 times (18 sts).

Rnd 18: (Dec, sc) 6 times (12 sts).

Rnd 19: Dec 6 times (6 sts).

Fasten off and sew the hole closed.

Ears (make 2)

With MC, make a MR, then sc 6 into the MR (6 sts).

Rnd 1: Sc in each st (6 sts).

Rnd 2: With MC, inc. With C1, sc 1. With MC, sc 1, inc, sc 2 (8 sts).

Rnd 3: With MC, sc 2. With C1, sc 2. With MC, sc 4 (8 sts).

Rnd 4: With MC, inc, sc. With C1, sc 2, inc. With MC, sc 3 (10 sts).

Rnd 5: With MC, inc, sc 2. With C1, sc 2, inc, sc 2. With MC, sc 2 (12 sts).

Fasten off and leave a 12-inch (30.5-cm) tail for sewing.

Assembly

Sew each Ear onto Rnd 12 of the Head, 4 sts apart. Sew the Tail on the back of Rnd 20 of the Body. Sew the Head onto the neck of the Body. If you aren't using safety eyes, embroider a pair of eyes onto Rnd 6 of the Head, 8 sts apart. Finally, embroider a triangle-shaped nose 2 Rnds tall and 3 sts wide at its widest point on the Head.

Georgi the Golden Retriever

When we think of a "good boy," these dogs take the cake. Golden retrievers are one of the most energetic and friendly dogs! These are such a popular breed, of course I had to add this iconic dog to the collection.

Skill Level

Beginner

Size

Approx 6 inches (15 cm) long, 7 inches (18 cm) wide, and 10 inches (25.5 cm) tall

Yarn

Super chunky chenille yarn, Premier Yarns Parfait Chunky, 100% polyester, 131 yards (120 m), 3.5 oz (100 g)

- Mustard, 393 yds (360 m)

Hooks

US size H-8 (5mm)

Notions

Polyester fiberfill

Removable stitch marker used to mark the first stitch of the round (and other indicated stitches within a round)

Tapestry needle

Pair of 6-mm safety eyes (optional)

Gauge

20 sc x 18 rounds = 4 inches (10 cm)

Abbreviations

Ch(s) = chain(s)

Dec = decrease (crochet 2 sc together)

Flo = front loop only

Inc = increase (work 2 sc into one stitch)

MR = magic ring

Sc = single crochet

Sl st = slip stitch

St(s) = stitch(es)

Georgi the Golden Retriever Pattern

Legs (make 4)

Make a MR, then sc 8 into the MR (8 sts).

Rnd 1: Inc in each st (16 sts).

Rnds 2–3 (2 Rnds): Sc in each st (16 sts).

Rnd 4: Sc 4, dec 6 times (10 sts).

Rnds 5–9 (5 Rnds): Sc in each st (10 sts).

Sl st into the 1st st of Rnd 9.

Fasten off and leave a 3-inch (7.5-cm) tail.

Tail

Make a MR, then sc 8 into the MR (8 sts).

Rnds 1–10 (10 Rnds): Sc in each st (8 sts).

Fasten off and leave a 12-inch (30.5-cm) tail for sewing.

Body

With C1, ch 16. Inc in the 2nd chain from hook, and sc in the next 13 chs. Inc 2 times in the last ch. Rotate your work clockwise 180 degrees, so that you can work along the opposite side of the chain. Sc in the next 13 chs, and inc in the last ch (34 sts).

Rnd 1: Inc 2 times, sc 13, inc 4 times, sc 13, inc 2 times (42 sts).

Rnd 2: Sc 2. Attach Leg 1 by placing your hook into the 8th st of the Leg and the next st of the Body. Sc the sts together. Sc the 7th st of the Leg and the next st of the Body. Sc the 6th st of the Leg and the next st of the Body together. Sc 12. Attach Leg 2 the same way the first Leg was attached. Sc 3. Attach Leg 3 by placing your hook into the 1st st of the Leg and the next st of the Body. Sc the sts together. Sc the 2nd st of the Leg and the next st of the Body together. Sc the 3rd st of the Leg and the next st of the Body together. Sc 12. Attach the last Leg the same way the previous Leg was attached. Sc in the last st (42 sts).

Rnd 3: Sc into the first 2 sts of the Body. Sc into the remaining 7 sts of Leg 1. Sc into the next 12 sts of the Body. Sc into the remaining 7 sts of Leg 2. Sc into the next 3 sts of the Body. Sc into the remaining 7 sts of Leg 3. Sc into the next 12 sts of the Body. Sc into the remaining 7 sts of Leg 4. Sc into the remaining st of the Body (58 sts).

Rnds 4–14 (11 Rnds): Sc in each st (58 sts). Stuff the Legs on Rnd 8.

Rnd 15: Sc 19, (dec, sc 3) 6 times, sc 9 (52 sts).

Rnd 16: Sc in each st (52 sts). Stuff the Body.

Rnd 17: Sc 20, (dec, sc 2) 6 times, sc 8 (46 sts).

Rnd 18: Sc 39. Place a st marker in the 22nd st. Place your hook into the next st of the Body and the marked st. Sl st the sts together. Repeat this process with the next st of the Body and the 21st st, the next st of the Body and the 20th st, the next st of the Body and the 19th st, the next st of the Body and the 18th st, and the next st of the Body and the 17th st. (You will now have 12 sts connected in the middle of the Body, and 2 openings, with 17 sts each.) Sc into the last st of the Body (40 sts). Remove the st marker. For more info on this section, refer to Blake the Boxer on page 49.

Rnd 19: Sc 16. Place your hook into the last st of the Rnd, and sc into the st (17 sts).

Rnds 20–22 (3 Rnds): Sc in each st (17 sts).

Fasten off and leave a 12-inch (30.5-cm) tail for sewing.

To finish the Body, place your hook into the 23rd st of Rnd 18. Sc into the same st. Work into the remaining 16 sts by dec 8 times (9 sts).

Rnd 23: (Dec, sc) 3 times (6 sts).

Fasten off and sew the hole closed.

Head

Make a MR, then sc 8 into the MR (8 sts).

Rnd 1: Sc 3 times in the 1st st, sc 2, inc, sc 2, sc 3 in the next st, sc in the last st (13 sts).

Rnd 2: Sc, sc 3 times in the next st, sc 3, inc in the next 2 sts, sc 3, sc 3 times in the next st, sc 2 (19 sts).

Rnds 3–4 (2 Rnds): Sc in each st (19 sts).

Rnd 5: Sc 7. Inc in the next 5 sts, in the flo. In both loops, sc 7 (24 sts).

Rnd 6: Sc 8, (inc, sc) 4 times, sc 8 (28 sts).

Rnd 7: Sc 6, (inc, sc 3) 4 times, sc 6 (32 sts). Attach safety eyes 8 sts apart.

Rnds 8–15 (8 Rnds): Sc in each st (32 sts).

Rnd 16: (Dec, sc 2) 8 times (24 sts). Stuff the Head.

Rnd 17: Sc in each st (24 sts).

Rnd 18: (Dec, sc 2) 6 times (18 sts).

Rnd 19: (Dec, sc) 6 times (12 sts).

Rnd 20: Dec 6 times (6 sts).

Fasten off and sew the hole closed.

Ears (make 2)

Make a MR, then sc 6 into the MR (6 sts).

Rnd 1: Sc in each st (6 sts).

Rnd 2: (Inc, sc 2) 2 times (8 sts).

Rnd 3: Sc in each st (8 sts).

Rnd 4: (Inc, sc 3) 2 times (10 sts).

Rnd 5: (Inc, sc 4) 2 times (12 sts).

Rnd 6: (Inc, sc 2) 4 times (16 sts).

Rnds 7–10 (4 Rnds): Sc in each st (16 sts).

Fasten off and leave a 12-inch (30.5-cm) tail for sewing.

Assembly

Sew each Ear onto Rnd 12 of the Head, 4 sts apart, making sure that they are pointing down toward the ground. Sew the Tail on the back of Rnd 20 of the Body. Sew the Head onto the neck of the Body (Rnd 22). If you aren't using safety eyes, embroider a pair of eyes onto Rnd 7 of the Head, 8 sts apart. Finally, embroider a triangle-shaped nose 2 Rnds tall and 3 sts wide at its widest point on the Head.

Gina the German Shepherd

This breed has served in both World Wars! German shepherds are very loyal dogs—and so are their owners. You can even match your own German shepherd's coloring with the pattern to create a mini-sized replica!

Skill Level

Intermediate

Size

Approx 6 inches (15 cm) long, 7 inches (18 cm) wide, and 10 inches (25.5 cm) tall

Yarn

Super chunky chenille yarn, Premier Yarns Parfait Chunky, 100% polyester, 131 yards (120 m), 3.5 oz (100 g)

- Mustard (MC), 393 yds (360 m)
- Black (C1), 131 yds (120 m)

Hooks

US size H-8 (5mm)

Notions

Polyester fiberfill

Removable stitch marker used to mark the first stitch of the round (and other indicated stitches within a round)

Tapestry needle

Pair of 6-mm safety eyes (optional)

Gauge

20 sc x 18 rounds = 4 inches (10 cm)

Abbreviations

C1 = color 1

Ch(s) = chain(s)

Dec = decrease (crochet 2 sc together)

Inc = increase (work 2 sc into one stitch)

MC = main color

MR = magic ring

Sc = single crochet

Sl st = slip stitch

St(s) = stitch(es)

Gina the German Shepherd Pattern

Legs (make 4)

With MC, make a MR, then sc 8 into the MR (8 sts).

Rnd 1: Inc in each st (16 sts).

Rnds 2–3 (2 Rnds): Sc in each st (16 sts).

Rnd 4: Sc 4, dec 6 times (10 sts).

Rnds 5–7 (3 Rnds): Sc in each st (10 sts).

Sl st into the 1st st of Rnd 7.

Fasten off and leave a 3-inch (7.5-cm) tail. Set aside.

Tail

With C1, make a MR, then sc 8 into the MR (8 sts).

Rnds 1–4 (4 Rnds): Sc in each st (8 sts). Break C1.

Rnds 5–12 (8 Rnds): With MC, sc in each st (8 sts). Do not stuff.

Fasten off and leave a 12-inch (30.5-cm) tail for sewing.

Body

With MC, ch 16.

Inc in the 2nd chain from hook, sc in the next 13 chs, and inc 2 times in the last ch. Turn your work clockwise 180 degrees, so that you can work along the opposite side of the chain. Then, sc in the next 13 chs, and inc in the last ch (34 sts).

Rnd 1: Inc in the first 2 sts, sc 13, inc in the next 4 sts, sc 13, inc in the last 2 sts (42 sts).

Rnd 2: Sc 2. Attach Leg 1 by placing your hook into the 6th st of the Leg and the next st of the Body. Sc the sts together. Sc the 5th st of the Leg and the next st of the Body. Sc the 4th st of the Leg and the next st of the Body together. Sc 12. Attach Leg 2 the same way the first Leg was attached. Sc 3. Attach the third Leg by placing your hook into the 1st st of the Leg and the next st of the Body. Sc the sts together. Sc the 10th st of the Leg and the next st of the Body together. Sc the 9th st of the Leg and the next st of the Body together. Sc 12. Attach the last Leg the same way the previous Leg was attached. Sc in the last st (42 sts).

Rnd 3: Sc 2. Sc into the remaining 7 sts of Leg 1. Sc into the next 12 sts of the Body. Sc into the remaining 7 sts of Leg 2. Sc into the next 3 sts of the Body. Sc into the remaining 7 sts of Leg 3. Sc into the next 12 sts of the Body. Sc into the remaining 7 sts of Leg 4. Sc into the remaining st of the Body (58 sts).

Rnds 4–11 (8 Rnds): Sc in each st (58 sts).

Rnd 12: With MC, sc 13. With C1, sc 41. With MC, sc 4 (58 sts).

Rnd 13: With MC, sc 13. With C1, sc 42. With MC, sc 3 (58 sts).

Rnd 14: With MC, sc 14. With C1, sc 41. With MC, sc 3 (58 sts).

Rnd 15: With MC, sc 14. With C1, sc 6, (dec, sc 3) 6 times, sc 6. With MC, sc 2 (52 sts). Stuff the Legs.

Rnd 16: With MC, sc 15. With C1, sc 35. With MC, sc 2 (52 sts). Start to stuff the Body.

Rnd 17: With MC, sc 15. With C1, sc 5, (dec, sc 2) 6 times, sc 7. With MC, sc in the last st (46 sts).

Rnd 18: With MC, sc 16. With C1, sc 23. Place a st marker in the 22nd st from the beginning of the round. Place your hook into the next st of the Body and the st marker st. Sl st the sts together. Repeat this process with the next st of the Body and the 21st st, the next st of the Body and the 20th st, the next st of the Body and the 19th st, the next st of the Body and the 18th st, and the next st of the Body and the 17th st. (You will now have 12 sts connected in the middle of the Body, and 2 openings, with 17 sts each.) With C1, sc into the last st of the Body (40 sts). Break C1. Remove the st marker. For more info on this section, refer to Blake the Boxer on page 49.

Rnd 19: With MC, sc 16. Sc in the last st (17 sts).

Rnd 20: Sc in each st (17 sts).

Fasten off and leave a 12-inch (30.5-cm) tail for sewing.

To finish the Body, with MC, place your hook into the 23rd st of Rnd 18. Sc into the same st. Work into the remaining 16 sts by dec 8 times (9 sts). Finish stuffing the Body.

Rnd 21: (Dec, sc) 3 times (6 sts).

Fasten off and sew the hole closed.

Head

With C1, ch 5.

Inc in the 2nd chain from hook, sc in the next 2 chs, and inc 2 times in the last ch. Turn your work clockwise 180 degrees, so that you can work along the opposite side of the chain. Then, sc in the next 2 chs, and inc in the last ch (12 sts).

Rnd 1: Inc 2, sc 2, inc 4 times, sc 2, inc 2 (20 sts).

Rnds 2–4 (3 Rnds): Sc in each st (20 sts).

Rnd 5: With C1, sc 11. With MC, sc 1. With C1, sc 8 (20 sts).

Rnd 6: With C1, sc 10, inc. With MC, inc 2 times. With C1, inc, sc 2. With MC, sc 4 (24 sts).

Rnd 7: With MC, (inc, sc 3) 2 times, inc. With C1, sc 3, inc. With MC, sc 3. With C1, inc, sc 3. With MC, inc, sc 3 (30 sts).

Rnd 8: With MC, sc 13. With C1, sc 4. With MC, sc 4. With C1, sc 4. With MC, sc 5 (30 sts). Attach safety eyes on this round, 8 sts apart.

Rnd 9: With MC, sc 15. With C1, sc 2. With MC, sc 5. With C1, sc 2. With MC, sc 6 (30 sts). Break C1.

Rnds 10–15 (6 Rnds): With MC, sc in each st (30 sts).

Rnd 16: (Dec, sc 3) 6 times (24 sts). Stuff the Head.

Rnd 17: Sc in each st (24 sts).

Rnd 18: (Dec, sc 2) 6 times (18 sts).

Rnd 19: (Dec, sc) 6 times (12 sts).

Rnd 20: Dec 6 times (6 sts).

Fasten off and sew the hole closed.

Ears (make 2)

With C1, make a MR, then sc 6 into the MR (6 sts).

Rnd 1: (With C1, inc. With MC, sc 2) twice (8 sts).

Rnd 2: (With C1, sc 2. With MC, sc 2) twice (8 sts).

Rnd 3: (With MC, inc. With C1, sc 1. With MC, sc 2) twice (10 sts).

Rnd 4: (With MC, sc 2. With C1, sc. With MC, sc 2) twice (10 sts).

Rnd 5: (With MC, inc, sc. With C1, sc 1. With MC, sc 2) twice (12 sts).

Rnd 6: (With MC, inc, sc 2. With C1, sc 1. With MC, sc 2) twice (14 sts).

Rnd 7: (With MC, inc, sc 3. With C1, sc 1. With MC, sc 2) twice (16 sts).

Fasten off and leave a 12-inch (30.5-cm) tail for sewing.

Assembly

Sew each Ear onto Rnd 12 of the Head, 4 sts apart. Sew the Tail on the back of Rnd 20 of the Body. Sew the Head onto the neck of the Body. If you aren't using safety eyes, embroider a pair of eyes onto Rnd 6 of the Head, 8 sts apart. Finally, embroider a triangle-shaped nose 2 Rnds tall and 3 sts wide at its widest point on the Head.

Yunus the Yorkshire Terrier

Everyone knows that the smaller the dog, the quirkier their personality. These fluffy dogs are so small, but their personality is the opposite! The terrier takes some patience to work up because we use a special stitch to recreate the fluffiness of the fur.

Skill Level

Advanced

Size

Approx 6 inches (15 cm) long, 7 inches (18 cm) wide, and 10 inches (25.5 cm) tall

Yarn

Super chunky chenille yarn, Premier Yarns Parfait Chunky, 100% polyester, 131 yards (120 m), 3.5 oz (100 g)

- Toffee (MC), 393 yds (360 m)
- Gray (C1), 131 yds (120 m)

Hooks

US size H-8 (5mm)

Notions

Polyester fiberfill

Removable stitch marker used to mark the first stitch of the round (and other indicated stitches within a round)

Tapestry needle

Pair of 6-mm safety eyes (optional)

Gauge

20 sc x 18 rounds = 4 inches (10 cm)

Abbreviations

C1 = color 1
Ch(s) = chain(s)
Dec = decrease (crochet 2 sc together)
Flo = front loop only
Inc = increase (work 2 sc into one stitch)
MC = main color
MR = magic ring
Sc = single crochet
Sl st = slip stitch
St(s) = stitch(es)

Special Stitches

Loop Stitch (loop st): Place your hook into the next st, yarn over, and draw a loop. Remove the loop from your hook, place your hook into the front loop of the stitch, yarn over, and draw a loop. Yarn over, and pull through the remaining two loops on your hook. See page 8 for a photo tutorial of this stitch.

Yunus the Yorkshire Terrier Pattern

Legs (make 4)

With MC, make a MR, then sc 8 into the MR (8 sts).

Rnd 1: Inc 6 times (16 sts).

Rnds 2–3 (2 Rnds): Sc in each st (16 sts).

Rnd 4: Sc 4, dec 6 times (10 sts).

Rnds 5–7 (3 Rnds): Sc in each st (10 sts).

Sl st into the 1st st of Rnd 7.

Fasten off and leave a short tail. Set aside.

Tail

With MC, make a MR, then sc 8 into the MR (8 sts).

Rnds 1–4 (4 Rnds): Sc in each st (8 sts).

Fasten off and leave a 12-inch (30.5-cm) tail for sewing.

Body

With MC, ch 16. Inc in the 2nd chain from hook, sc in the next 13 chs, and inc 2 times in the last ch. Turn your work clockwise 180 degrees, so that you can work along the opposite side of the chain. Then, sc in the next 13 chs, and inc in the last ch (34 sts).

Rnd 1: Inc 2 times, sc 13, inc 4 times, sc 13, inc 2 times (42 sts).

Rnd 2: Sc 2. Attach a Leg by placing your hook into the 6th st of the Leg and the next st of the Body. Sc the sts together. Sc the 5th st of the Leg and the next st of the Body. Sc the 4th st of the Leg and the next st of the Body together. Sc 12. Attach a Leg the same way the first Leg was attached. Sc 3. Attach the third Leg by placing your hook into the 1st st of the Leg and the next st of the Body. Sc the sts together. Sc the 10th st of the Leg and the next st of the Body together. Sc the 9th st of the Leg and the next st of the Body together. Sc 12. Attach the last Leg the same way the previous Leg was attached. Sc in the last st (42 sts).

Rnd 3: Sc into the first 2 sts of the Body. Sc into the remaining 7 sts of Leg 1. Sc into the next 12 sts of the Body. Sc into the remaining 7 sts of Leg 2. Sc into the next 3 sts of the Body. Sc into the remaining 7 sts of Leg 3. Sc into the next 12 sts of the Body. Sc into the remaining 7 sts of Leg 4. Sc into the remaining st of the Body (58 sts).

Rnd 4: With MC, sc 11. With C1, sc 38. With MC, sc 9 (58 sts).

Rnd 5: With MC, sc 12. With C1, sc 37. With MC, sc 9 (58 sts).

Rnd 6: With MC, sc 12. With C1, sc 38. With MC, sc 8 (58 sts).

Rnd 7: With MC, sc 10. With C1, sc 42. With MC, sc 6 (58 sts).

Rnd 8: With MC, sc 11. With C1, sc 41. With MC, sc 6 (58 sts).

Rnd 9: With MC, sc 11. With C1, sc 42. With MC, sc 5 (58 sts).

Rnd 10: With MC, sc 12. With C1, sc 41. With MC, sc 5 (58 sts).

Rnd 11: With MC, sc 12. With C1, sc 42. With MC, sc 4 (58 sts).

Rnd 12: With MC, sc 13. With C1, sc 41. With MC, sc 4 (58 sts).

Rnd 13: With MC, sc 13. With C1, sc 42. With MC, sc 3 (58 sts).

Rnd 14: With MC, sc 14. With C1, sc 41. With MC, sc 3 (58 sts).

Rnd 15: With MC, sc 14. With C1, sc 6, (dec, sc 3) 6 times, sc 6. With MC, sc 2 (52 sts).

Rnd 16: With MC, sc 15. With C1, sc 35. With MC, sc 2 (52 sts).

Rnd 17: With MC, sc 15. With C1, sc 5, (dec, sc 2) 6 times, sc 7. With MC, sc (46 sts).

Rnd 18: With MC, sc 16. With C1, sc 23. Place a st marker in the 22nd st from the beginning of the round. Place your hook into the next st of the Body and the st marker st. Sl st the sts together. Repeat this process with the next st of the Body and the 21st st, the next st of the Body and the 20th st, the next st of the Body and the 19th st, the next st of the Body and the 18th st, and the next st of the Body and the 17th st. (You will now have 12 sts connected in the middle of the Body, and 2 openings, with 17 sts each.) With MC, sc into the last st of the Body (40 sts). Break C1. Remove the st marker. For more info on this section, refer to Blake the Boxer on page 49.

Rnd 19: With MC, sc 16. Place your hook into the last st of the Rnd, and sc into the st (17 sts).

Rnd 20: Sc in each st (17 sts).

Fasten off and leave a 12-inch (30.5-cm) tail for sewing.

(Rnd 20 continued)

To finish the Body, place your hook into the 23rd st of Rnd 18. Sc into the same st. Work into the remaining 16 sts by dec 8 times (9 sts).

Rnd 21: (Dec, sc) 3 times (6 sts).

Fasten off and sew the hole closed.

Head

With MC, make a MR and sc 8 into the MR (8 sts).

Rnd 1: Inc 8 times (16 sts).

Rnd 2: Sc 3, loop st 4 times, sc 5, loop st 4 times (16 sts).

Rnd 3: Sc 3, loop st 5 times, sc 5, loop st 3 times (16 sts).

Rnd 4: Sc 4, loop st 4 times, sc 5, loop st 3 times (16 sts).

Rnd 5: Sc 7. In the flo, inc 3 times, sc 2, inc 3 times, sc 1 (22 sts).

Rnd 6: Sc 7, (inc, sc) 3 times, sc 2, (inc, sc) 3 times, sc 1 (28 sts). If using, attach safety eyes on this Rnd, 7 sts apart.

Rnd 7: Sc in each st (28 sts).

Rnd 8: Sc 6, (sc 2, inc) 2 times, sc 6, (inc, sc 2) 3 times, sc 2 (34 sts).

Rnd 9: Sc 15, loop st 4 times, sc 3, loop st 4 times, sc 8 (34 sts).

Rnd 10: Sc 16, loop st 3 times, sc 4, loop st 3 times, sc 8 (34 sts).

Rnds 11–12 (2 Rnds): Sc in each st (34 sts).

Rnd 13: Sc 9, (dec, sc 2) 3 times, sc 5, (dec, sc 2) 2 times (29 sts).

Rnd 14: Dec, sc 27 (28 sts).

Rnd 15: Sc in each st (28 sts).

Rnd 16: Sc 11, (dec, sc) 5 times, dec (22 sts).

Rnd 17: (Dec, sc 3, dec, sc 4) 2 times (18 sts).

Rnd 18: (Dec, sc) 6 times (12 sts).

Rnd 19: Dec 6 times (6 sts).

Fasten off and sew the hole closed.

Ears (make 2)

With MC, make a MR and sc 6 into the MR (6 sts).

Rnd 1: Sc in each st (6 sts).

Rnd 2: With MC, inc. With C1, sc. With MC, sc, inc, sc 2 (8 sts).

Rnd 3: With MC, sc 2. With C1, sc 2. With MC, sc 4 (8 sts).

Rnd 4: With MC, inc, sc. With C1, sc 2, inc. With MC, sc 3 (10 sts).

Rnd 5: With MC, inc, sc 2. With C1, sc 2, inc, sc 2. With MC, sc 2 (12 sts).

Fasten off and leave a 12-inch (30.5-cm) tail for sewing.

Assembly

Sew each Ear onto Rnd 12 of the Head, 4 sts apart. Sew the Tail on the back of Rnd 20 of the Body. Sew the Head onto the neck of the Body. If you aren't using safety eyes, embroider a pair of eyes onto Rnd 6 of the Head, 8 sts apart. Finally, embroider a triangle-shaped nose 2 Rnds tall and 3 sts wide at its widest point on the Head.

Dale the Doberman

At first glance, these dogs can look very intimidating. However, even though dobermans are so big, they are a very sweet breed! When you're crocheting your doberman, try crocheting one ear up and one ear down to show some personality.

Skill Level

Intermediate

Size

Approx 6 inches (15 cm) long, 7 inches (18 cm) wide, and 10 inches (25.5 cm) tall

Yarn

Super chunky chenille yarn, Premier Yarns Parfait Chunky, 100% polyester, 131 yards (120 m), 3.5 oz (100 g)

- Black (MC), 393 yds (360 m)
- Teddy Bear (C1), 131 yds (120 m)

Hooks

US size H-8 (5mm)

Notions

Polyester fiberfill

Removable stitch marker used to mark the first stitch of the round (and other indicated stitches within a round)

Tapestry needle

Pair of 6-mm safety eyes (optional)

Gauge

20 sc x 18 rounds = 4 inches (10 cm)

Abbreviations

C1 = color 1

Ch(s) = chain(s)

Dec = decrease (crochet 2 sc together)

Flo = front loop only

Inc = increase (work 2 sc into one stitch)

MC = main color

MR = magic ring

Sc = single crochet

Sl st = slip stitch

St(s) = stitch(es)

Dale the Doberman Pattern

Tail

With MC, make a MR, then sc 8 into the MR (8 sts).

Rnds 1–10 (10 Rnds): Sc in each st (8 sts).

Fasten off and leave a 12-inch (30.5-cm) tail for sewing.

Front Legs (make 2)

With C1, make a MR, then sc 8 into the MR (8 sts).

Rnd 1: Inc in each st (16 sts).

Rnds 2–3 (2 Rnds): Sc in each st (16 sts).

Rnd 4: Sc 4, dec 6 times (10 sts).

Rnds 5–7 (3 Rnds): Sc in each st (10 sts).

Sl st into the 1st st of Rnd 7. Do not stuff.

Fasten off and leave a 3-inch (7.5-cm) tail. Set aside.

Back Legs (make 2)

Repeat Rnds 1–7 of the Front Leg. Stuff the Leg before you continue. (Only Rnds 1–7 will be stuffed.) Break C1.

Rnd 8: With MC, sc 5. Inc 5 times in the flo (15 sts).

Rnd 9: Inc 2 times in the flo. In both loops, sc 13 (17 sts).

Rnds 10–13 (4 Rnds): Sc in each st (17 sts).

Rnd 14: Dec 8, sc (9 sts).

Fasten off and leave a 12-inch (30.5-cm) tail for sewing. Sew the hole closed. Set aside.

Body

With MC, make a MR, then sc 8 into the MR (8 sts).

Rnd 1: Inc in each st (16 sts).

Rnd 2: (Inc, sc) 8 times (24 sts).

Rnd 3: (Inc, sc 2) 8 times (32 sts).

Rnd 4: (Inc, sc 3) 8 times (40 sts).

Rnd 5: (Inc, sc 4) 8 times (48 sts).

Rnd 6: (Inc, sc 5) 8 times (56 sts).

Rnds 7–10 (4 Rnds): Sc in each st (56 sts).

Rnd 11: Sc 24, (dec, sc 2) 8 times (48 sts).

Rnd 12: Sc 8. Attach a Front Leg by placing your hook into the 5th st of the Leg and the next st of the Body. Sc the sts together. Sc the 4th st of the Leg and the next st of the Body. Sc the 3rd st of the Leg and the next st of the Body together. Sc 2. Attach the 2nd Front Leg the same way as the previous Leg.
Sc 32 (48 sts).

Rnd 13: Sc into the next 8 sts of the Body. Sc into the remaining 7 sts of the Leg. Sc into the next 2 sts of the Body. Sc into the remaining 7 sts of the Leg. Sc into the remaining 32 sts of the Body (56 sts).

Rnds 14–15 (2 Rnds): Sc in each st (56 sts).

Rnd 16: Sc 29, (dec, sc 3) 5 times, dec in last 2 sts (50 sts). Start to stuff the Legs and Body.

Rnd 17: Sc 8, dec, sc 15, dec, sc 23 (48 sts).

Rnd 18: Sc 26, (sc 2, dec) 5 times, dec (42 sts).

Rnd 19: With MC, sc 7, dec, sc 2. With C1, sc 3. With MC, sc 7. With C1, sc, dec, sc. With MC, sc 17 (40 sts).

Rnd 20: With MC, sc 10. With C1, sc 3. With MC, sc 7. With C1, sc 3. With MC, sc 17 (40 sts).

Rnd 21: With MC, sc 11. With C1, sc 2. With MC, sc 8. With C1, sc 2. With MC, sc 17 (40 sts). Break C1.

Rnd 22: With MC, sc 23, (sc, dec) 5 times, dec in last 2 sts (34 sts). Continue to stuff the Legs and Body.

Rnd 23: Sc 7, dec, sc 12, dec, sc 11 (32 sts).

Rnd 24: Sc in each st (32 sts). Finish stuffing the Legs and Body.

Rnd 25: Sc 22, dec 5 (27 sts).

Rnd 26: Dec 3 times, sc 21 (24 sts).

Rnds 27–28 (2 Rnds): Sc in each st (24 sts).

Fasten off and leave a 12-inch (30.5-cm) tail for sewing.

Head

With C1, make a MR, then sc 8 into the MR (8 sts).

Rnd 1: Sc 3 times in the 1st st, sc 2, inc, sc 2, sc 3 in the next st, sc in the last st (13 sts).

Rnd 2: Sc, sc 3 times in the next st, sc 3, inc in the next 2 sts, sc 3, sc 3 times in the next st, sc 2 (19 sts).

Rnds 3–4 (2 Rnds): Sc in each st (19 sts).

Rnd 5: With C1, sc 7. With MC, inc in the next 5 sts, in the flo. With C1, in both loops, sc 7 (24 sts).

Rnd 6: With C1, sc 7. With MC, (sc, inc) 5 times, sc 2. With C1, sc 4 (28 sts).

Rnd 7: With C1, sc 6, inc. With MC, sc 3, (inc, sc 3) 3 times. With C1, sc 6 (32 sts). If using, attach safety eyes on this Rnd, 8 sts apart.

Rnd 8: With C1, sc 8. With MC, sc 18. With C1, sc 6 (32 sts).

Rnd 9: With C1, sc 8. With MC, sc 21. With C1, sc 3 (32 sts). Start to stuff the Head.

Rnd 10: With C1, sc 8. With MC, sc 23. With C1, sc 1 (32 sts).

Rnd 11: With C1, sc 7. With MC, sc 25 (32 sts).

Rnd 12: With MC, sc 1. With C1, sc 5. With MC, sc 26 (32 sts). Break C1.

Rnds 13–15 (3 Rnds): With MC, sc in each st (32 sts).

Rnd 16: (Dec, sc 2) 8 times (24 sts). Stuff the Head.

Rnd 17: Sc in each st (24 sts).

Rnd 18: (Dec, sc 2) 6 times (18 sts).

Rnd 19: (Dec, sc) 6 times (12 sts).

Rnd 20: Dec 6 times (6 sts).

Fasten off and sew the hole closed.

Ears (make 2)

With MC, make a MR and sc 6 into the MR (6 sts).

Rnd 1: Sc in each st (6 sts).

Rnd 2: (Inc, sc 2) 2 times (8 sts).

Rnd 3: Sc in each st (8 sts).

Rnd 4: (Inc, sc 3) 2 times (10 sts).

Rnd 5: (Inc, sc 4) 2 times (12 sts).

Rnd 6: (Inc, sc 2) 4 times (16 sts).

Rnds 7–10 (4 Rnds): Sc in each st (16 sts).

Fasten off and leave a 12-inch (30.5-cm) tail for sewing.

Assembly

Sew each Ear onto Rnd 12 of the Head, 4 sts apart. Make sure the Ears are pointing upward. Sew each Back Leg onto Rnd 7 of the Body, beside each Front Leg. Sew the Tail onto the back of the Body on Rnd 20. Sew the Head onto the neck of the Body. If you aren't using safety eyes, embroider a pair of eyes onto Rnd 7 of the Head, 8 sts apart. Finally, embroider a triangle-shaped nose 2 Rnds tall and 3 sts wide at its widest point on the Head.

Blake the Boxer

It's important to get a pet that matches your lifestyle. Boxers are the "clowns" of the dog world due to their energetic nature! If you're as energetic and lighthearted as this breed, this pattern will be incredibly fun to work up.

Skill Level

Intermediate

Size

Approx 6 inches (15 cm) long, 7 inches (18 cm) wide, and 10 inches (25.5 cm) tall

Yarn

Super chunky chenille yarn, Premier Yarns Parfait Chunky, 100% polyester, 131 yards (120 m), 3.5 oz (100 g)

- Teddy Bear (MC), 393 yds (360 m)
- Cream (C1), 131 yds (120 m)
- Black (C2), 5 yds (5 m)

Hooks

US size H-8 (5mm)

Notions

Polyester fiberfill

Removable stitch marker used to mark the first stitch of the round (and other indicated stitches within a round)

Tapestry needle

Pair of 6-mm safety eyes (optional)

Gauge

20 sc x 18 rounds = 4 inches (10 cm)

Abbreviations

C1 = color 1

C2 = color 2

Ch(s) = chain(s)

Dec = decrease (crochet 2 sc together)

Flo = front loop only

Inc = increase (work 2 sc into one stitch)

MC = main color

MR = magic ring

Sc = single crochet

Sl st = slip stitch

St(s) = stitch(es)

Blake the Boxer Pattern

Legs (make 4)

With C1, make a MR, then sc 8 into the MR (8 sts).

Rnd 1: Inc in each st (16 sts).

Rnds 2–3 (2 Rnds): Sc in each st (16 sts). Break C1.

Rnd 4: With MC, sc 4, dec 6 times (10 sts).

Rnds 5–7 (3 Rnds): Sc in each st (10 sts). Sl st into the 1st st of Rnd 7. Do not stuff.

Fasten off and leave a 3-inch (7.5-cm) tail. Set aside.

Tail

With C2, make a MR, then sc 8 into the MR (8 sts).

Rnds 1–4 (4 Rnds): Sc in each st (8 sts). Break C2.

Rnds 5–8 (4 Rnds): With MC, sc in each st (8 sts). Do not stuff.

Fasten off and leave a 12-inch (30.5-cm) tail for sewing. Set aside.

Body

With C1, ch 16.

Inc in the 2nd chain from hook, sc in the next 13 chs, and inc 2 times in the last ch. Turn your work clockwise 180 degrees, so that you can work along the opposite side of the chain. Then, sc in the next 13 chs, and inc in the last ch (34 sts).

Rnd 1: Inc in the 1st 2 sts, sc 13, inc in the next 4 sts, sc 13, inc in the last 2 sts (42 sts).

Rnd 2: Sc 2. Attach Leg 1 by placing your hook into the 6th st of the Leg and the next st of the Body. Sc the sts together. Sc the 5th st of the Leg and the next st of the Body. Sc the 4th st of the Leg and the next st of the Body together. Sc 12. Attach Leg 2 the same way the first Leg was attached. Sc 3. Attach the third Leg by placing your hook into the 1st st of the Leg and the next st of the Body. Sc the sts together. Sc the 10th st of the Leg and the next st of the Body together. Sc the 9th st of the Leg and the next st of the Body together. Sc 12. Attach the last Leg the same way the previous Leg was attached. Sc in the last st (42 sts).

Rnd 3: Sc 2. With MC, sc into the remaining 7 sts of Leg 1. Sc into the next 12 sts of the Body. Sc into the remaining 7 sts of Leg 2. Sc into the next 3 sts of the Body. Sc into the remaining 7 sts of Leg 3. Sc into the next 12 sts of the Body. Sc into the remaining 7 sts of Leg 4. With C1, sc into the remaining st of the Body (58 sts).

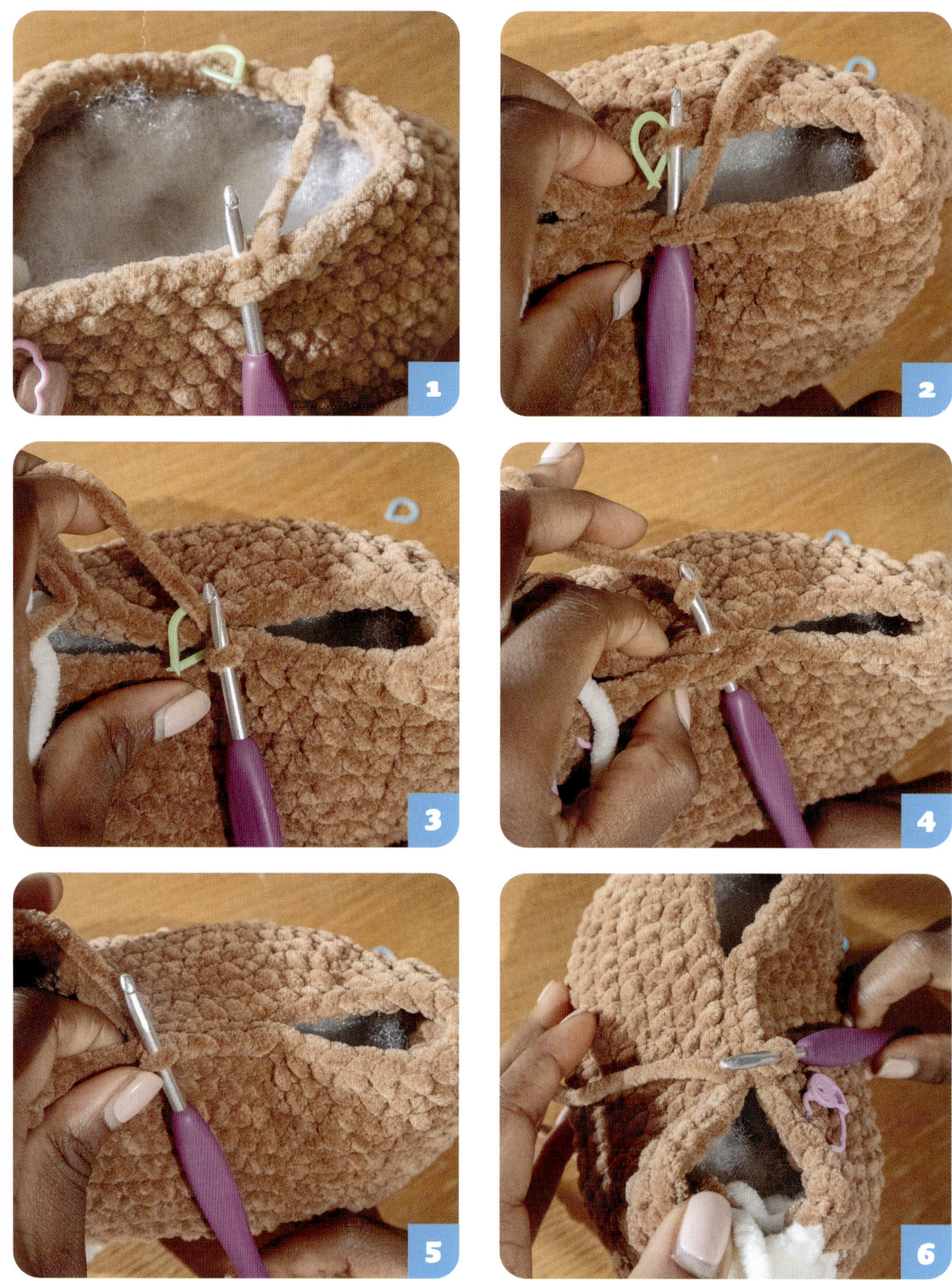
1
2
3
4
5
6

Rnd 4: With C1, sc 3. With MC, sc 53. With C1, sc 2 (58 sts).

Rnds 5–6 (2 Rnds): With C1, sc 4. With MC, sc 53. With C1, sc 1 (58 sts).

Rnds 7–8 (2 Rnds): With C1, sc 5. With MC, sc 53 (58 sts).

Rnd 9: With C1, sc 6. With MC, sc 52 (58 sts).

Rnd 10: With MC, sc 1. With C1, sc 5. With C1, sc 52 (58 sts).

Rnd 11: With MC, sc 1. With C1, sc 6. With MC, sc 51 (58 sts).

Rnd 12: With MC, sc 2. With C1, sc 5. With MC, sc 51 (58 sts).

Rnd 13: With MC, sc 2. With C1, sc 6. With MC, sc 50 (58 sts).

Rnd 14: With MC, sc 3. With C1, sc 5. With MC, sc 50 (58 sts).

Rnd 15: With MC, sc 3. With C1, sc 6. With MC, sc 11, (dec, sc 3) 6 times, sc 8 (52 sts). Stuff the Legs.

Rnd 16: With MC, sc 4. With C1, sc 5. With MC, sc 43 (52 sts). Start to stuff the Body.

Rnd 17: With MC, sc 4. With C1, sc 6. With MC, sc 10, (dec, sc 2) 6 times, sc 8 (46 sts).

Rnd 18: With MC, sc 5. With C1, sc 5. With MC, sc 29. Place a st marker in the 22nd st from the beginning of the round (image 1). Place your hook into the next st of the Body and the marked st (image 2). Sl st the sts together (image 3). Repeat this process with the next st of the Body and the 21st st (image 4), the next st of the Body and the 20th st, the next st of the Body and the 19th st, the next st of the Body and the 18th st, and the next st of the Body and the 17th st (image 5). You will now have 12 sts connected in the middle of the Body, and 2 openings, with 17 sts each (image 6). With MC, sc into the last st of the Body (40 sts). Break C1. Remove the st marker.

Rnd 19: With MC, sc 16. Sc in the last st (17 sts).

7
8
9
10

Rnd 20: Sc in each st (17 sts).

Fasten off and leave a 12-inch (30.5-cm) tail for sewing.

To finish the Body, with MC, place your hook into the 23rd st of Rnd 18 (image 7). Sc into the same st (images 8–9). Work into the remaining 16 sts by dec 8 times (image 10) (9 sts). Finish stuffing the Body.

Rnd 21: (Dec, sc) 3 times (6 sts).

Fasten off and sew the hole closed.

Head

With C1, ch 5.

Inc in the 2nd chain from hook, sc in the next 2 chs, and inc 2 times in the last ch. Turn your work clockwise 180 degrees, so that you can work along the opposite side of the chain. Then, sc in the next 2 chs, and inc in the last ch (12 sts).

Rnd 1: Inc 2, sc 2, inc 4 times, sc 2, inc 2 (20 sts).

Rnds 2–4 (3 Rnds): Sc in each st (20 sts).

Rnd 5: With C1, sc 15. With MC, sc 5 (20 sts).

Rnd 6: With MC, sc 9. With C1, sc, inc 4 times, sc. With MC, sc 5 (24 sts).

Rnd 7: With MC, (inc, sc 3) 2 times, inc. With C2, sc 3. With MC, inc. With C1, sc 3. With MC, inc. With C2, sc 3. With MC, inc, sc 3 (30 sts). Attach safety eyes 8 sts apart.

Rnd 8: With MC, sc 12. With C2, sc 4. With MC, sc 2. With C1, sc 2. With MC, sc 2. With C2, sc 4. With MC, sc 4 (30 sts).

Rnd 9: With MC, sc 12. With C2, sc 4. With MC, sc 3. With C1, sc 1. With MC, sc 3. With C2, sc 4. With MC, sc 3 (30 sts). Break C1.

Rnd 10: With MC, sc 13. With C2, sc 3. With MC, sc 8. With C2, sc 3. With MC, sc 3 (30 sts). Break C2.

Rnds 11–15 (5 Rnds): With MC, sc in each st (30 sts).

Rnd 16: (Dec, sc 3) 6 times (24 sts). Stuff the Head.

Rnd 17: Sc in each st (24 sts).

Rnd 18: (Dec, sc 2) 6 times (18 sts).

Rnd 19: (Dec, sc) 6 times (12 sts).

Rnd 20: Dec 6 times (6 sts).

Fasten off and sew the hole closed.

Ears (make 2)

With C2, make a MR and sc 6 into the MR (6 sts).

Rnd 1: Sc in each st (6 sts).

Rnd 2: (Inc, sc 2) 2 times (8 sts).

Rnd 3: Sc in each st (8 sts).

Rnd 4: (Inc, sc 3) 2 times (10 sts).

Rnd 5: (Inc, sc 4) 2 times (12 sts). Break C2.

Rnd 6: With MC, (inc, sc 2) 4 times (16 sts).

Rnds 7–10 (4 Rnds): Sc in each st (16 sts).

Fasten off and leave a 12-inch (30.5-cm) tail for sewing.

Assembly

Sew each Ear onto Rnd 12 of the Head, 4 sts apart. Sew the Tail on the back of Rnd 20 of the Body. Sew the Head onto the neck of the Body. If you aren't using safety eyes, embroider a pair of eyes onto Rnd 6 of the Head, 8 sts apart. Finally, embroider a triangle-shaped nose 2 Rnds tall and 3 sts wide at its widest point on the Head.

Bria the Beagle

Beagles are such fun-loving and easygoing dogs! These dogs like company, as they usually enjoy being in a pack. Consider making multiple beagles so that your first beagle plushie doesn't feel alone!

Skill Level

Intermediate

Size

Approx 6 inches (15 cm) long, 7 inches (18 cm) wide, and 10 inches (25.5 cm) tall

Yarn

Super chunky chenille yarn, Premier Yarns Parfait Chunky, 100% polyester, 131 yards (120 m), 3.5 oz (100 g)

- Mustard (MC), 393 yds (360 m)
- Cream (C1), 131 yds (120 m)
- Black (C2), 5 yds (5 m)

Hooks

US size H-8 (5mm)

Notions

Polyester fiberfill

Removable stitch marker used to mark the first stitch of the round (and other indicated stitches within a round)

Tapestry needle

Pair of 6-mm safety eyes (optional)

Gauge

20 sc x 18 rounds = 4 inches (10 cm)

Abbreviations

C1 = color 1

C2 = color 2

Ch(s) = chain(s)

Dec = decrease (crochet 2 sc together)

Inc = increase (work 2 sc into one stitch)

MC = main color

MR = magic ring

Sc = single crochet

Sl st = slip stitch

St(s) = stitch(es)

Bria the Beagle Pattern

Legs (make 4)

With C1, make a MR, then sc 8 into the MR (8 sts).

Rnd 1: Inc in each st (16 sts).

Rnds 2–3 (2 Rnds): Sc in each st (16 sts).

Rnd 4: Sc 4, dec 6 times (10 sts).

Rnds 5–7 (3 Rnds): Sc in each st (10 sts).

Sl st into the 1st st of Rnd 7.

Fasten off and leave a 3-inch (7.5-cm) tail. Set aside.

Tail

With C1, make a MR, then sc 8 into the MR (8 sts).

Rnds 1–4 (4 Rnds): Sc in each st (8 sts).

Rnds 5–8 (4 Rnds): With C2, sc in each st (8 sts). Do not stuff.

Fasten off and leave a 12-inch (30.5-cm) tail for sewing.

Body

With C1, ch 16.

Inc in the 2nd chain from hook, sc in the next 13 chs, and inc 2 times in the last ch. Turn your work clockwise 180 degrees, so that you can work along the opposite side of the chain. Then, sc in the next 13 chs, and inc in the last ch (34 sts).

Rnd 1: Inc in the 1st 2 sts, sc 13, inc in the next 4 sts, sc 13, inc in the last 2 sts (42 sts).

Rnd 2: Sc 2. Attach Leg 1 by placing your hook into the 6th st of the Leg and the next st of the Body. Sc the sts together. Sc the 5th st of the Leg and the next st of the Body. Sc the 4th st of the Leg and the next st of the Body together. Sc 12. Attach Leg 2 the same way the first Leg was attached. Sc 3. Attach Leg 3 by placing your hook into the 1st st of the Leg and the next st of the Body. Sc the sts together. Sc the 10th st of the Leg and the next st of the Body together. Sc the 9th st of the Leg and the next st of the Body together. Sc 12. Attach the last Leg the same way the previous Leg was attached. Sc in the last st (42 sts).

Rnd 3: Sc 2. Sc into the remaining 7 sts of Leg 1. Sc into the next 12 sts of the Body. Sc into the remaining 7 sts of Leg 2. Sc into the next 3 sts of the Body. Sc into the remaining 7 sts of Leg 3. Sc into the next 12 sts of the Body. Sc into the remaining 7 sts of Leg 4. Sc into the remaining st of the Body (58 sts).

Rnd 4: With C1, sc 11. With MC, sc 38. With C1, sc 9 (58 sts).

Rnd 5: With C1, sc 12. With MC, sc 37. With C1, sc 9 (58 sts).

Rnd 6: With C1, sc 12. With MC, sc 38. With C1, sc 8 (58 sts).

Rnd 7: With C1, sc 10. With MC, sc 42. With C1, sc 6 (58 sts).

Rnd 8: With C1, sc 11. With MC, sc 41. With C1, sc 6 (58 sts).

Rnd 9: With C1, sc 11. With MC, sc 42. With C1, sc 5 (58 sts).

Rnd 10: With C1, sc 12. With MC, sc 41. With C1, sc 5 (58 sts).

Rnd 11: With C1, sc 12. With MC, sc 42. With C1, sc 4 (58 sts). Break MC.

Rnd 12: With C1, sc 13. With C2, sc 41. With C1, sc 4 (58 sts).

Rnd 13: With C1, sc 13. With C2, sc 42. With C1, sc 3 (58 sts).

Rnd 14: With C1, sc 14. With C2, sc 41. With C1, sc 3 (58 sts).

Rnd 15: With C1, sc 14. With C2, sc 6, (dec, sc 3) 6 times, sc 6. With C1, sc 2 (52 sts). Stuff the Legs.

Rnd 16: With C1, sc 15. With C2, sc 35. With C1, sc 2 (52 sts). Start to stuff the Body.

Rnd 17: With C1, sc 15. With C2, sc 5, (dec, sc 2) 6 times, sc 7. With C1, sc in the last st (46 sts).

Rnd 18: With C1, sc 16. With C2, sc 23. Place a st marker in the 22nd st from the beginning of the round. Place your hook into the next st of the Body and the st marker st. Sl st the sts together. Repeat this process with the next st of the Body and the 21st st, the next st of the Body and the 20th st, the next st of the Body and the 19th st, the next st of the Body and the 18th st, and the next st of the Body and the 17th st. (You will now have 12 sts connected in the middle of the Body, and 2 openings, with 17 sts each.) With C1, sc into the last st of the Body (40 sts). Break C1. Remove the st marker. For more info on this section, refer to Blake the Boxer on page 49.

Rnd 19: With C2, sc 16. Sc in the last st (17 sts).

Rnd 20: Sc in each st (17 sts).

Fasten off and leave a 12-inch (30.5-cm) tail for sewing.

To finish the Body, with MC, place your hook into the 23rd st of Rnd 18. Sc into the same st. Work into the remaining 16 sts by dec 8 times (9 sts). Finish stuffing the Body.

Rnd 21: (Dec, sc) 3 times (6 sts).

Fasten off and sew the hole closed.

Head

With C1, ch 5.

Inc in the 2nd chain from hook, sc in the next 2 chs, and inc 2 times in the last ch. Turn your work clockwise 180 degrees, so that you can work along the opposite side of the chain. Then, sc in the next 2 chs, and inc in the last ch (12 sts).

Rnd 1: Inc 2, sc 2, inc 4 times, sc 2, inc 2 (20 sts).

Rnds 2–4 (3 Rnds): Sc in each st (20 sts).

Rnd 5: With C1, sc 15. With MC, sc 5 (20 sts).

Rnd 6: With C1, sc 9. With MC, sc, inc 4 times, sc. With C1, sc 5 (24 sts). Attach safety eyes to this Rnd, 8 sts apart.

Rnd 7: With MC, (inc, sc 3) 3 times, inc. With C1, sc 3. With MC, (inc, sc 3) 2 times (30 sts).

Rnd 8: With MC, sc 18. With C1, sc 2. With MC, sc 10 (30 sts).

Rnd 9: With MC, sc 19. With C1, sc 1. With MC, sc 10 (30 sts). Break C1.

Rnds 10–15 (6 Rnds): With MC, sc in each st (30 sts).

Rnd 16: (Dec, sc 3) 6 times (24 sts). Stuff the Head.

Rnd 17: Sc in each st (24 sts).

Rnd 18: (Dec, sc 2) 6 times (18 sts).

Rnd 19: (Dec, sc) 6 times (12 sts).

Rnd 20: Dec 6 times (6 sts).

Fasten off and sew the hole closed.

Ears (make 2)

With MC, make a MR, then sc 8 into the MR (8 sts).

Rnd 1: Inc in each st (16 sts).

Rnds 2–4 (3 Rnds): Sc in each st (16 sts).

Rnd 5: (Dec, sc 2) 4 times (12 sts).

Rnds 6–9 (4 Rnds): Sc in each st (12 sts).

Rnd 10: (Dec, sc) 4 times (8 sts).

Rnd 11: Sc in each st (8 sts).

Fasten off and leave a 12-inch (30.5-cm) tail for sewing.

Assembly

Sew each Ear onto Rnd 12 of the Head, 4 sts apart. Sew the Tail on the back of Rnd 20 of the Body. Sew the Head onto the neck of the Body. If you aren't using safety eyes, embroider a pair of eyes onto Rnd 6 of the Head, 8 sts apart. Finally, embroider a triangle-shaped nose 2 Rnds tall and 3 sts wide at its widest point on the Head.

Penny the Poodle

Poodles are high-maintenance dogs—but for good reason. Poodles are a truly regal breed, and their personality matches this perfectly! To add even more personality, try changing the color, or try making your poodle with fluffy yarn!

Skill Level

Intermediate

Size

Approx 6 inches (15 cm) long, 7 inches (18 cm) wide, and 10 inches (25.5 cm) tall

Yarn

Super chunky chenille yarn, Premier Yarns Parfait Chunky, 100% polyester, 131 yards (120 m), 3.5 oz (100 g)

- Cream, 393 yds (360 m)

Hooks

US size H-8 (5mm)

Notions

Polyester fiberfill

Removable stitch marker used to mark the first stitch of the round (and other indicated stitches within a round)

Tapestry needle

Pair of 6-mm safety eyes (optional)

Gauge

20 sc x 18 rounds = 4 inches (10 cm)

Abbreviations

Ch(s) = chain(s)

Dec = decrease (crochet 2 sc together)

Inc = increase (work 2 sc into one stitch)

MR = magic ring

Sc = single crochet

Sl st = slip stitch

St(s) = stitch(es)

Special Stitches

Loop Stitch (loop st): Place your hook into the next st, yarn over, and draw a loop. Remove the loop from your hook, place your hook into the front loop of the stitch, yarn over, and draw a loop. Yarn over, and pull through the remaining two loops on your hook. See page 8 for a photo tutorial of this stitch.

Penny the Poodle Pattern

Legs (make 4)

Make a MR, then sc 8 into the MR (8 sts).

Rnd 1: Inc in each st (16 sts).

Rnds 2–3 (2 Rnds): Sc in each st (16 sts).

Rnd 4: Sc 4, dec 6 times (10 sts).

Rnd 5: Loop st in each st (10 sts).

Rnd 6: Sc into each st (10 sts).

Rnd 7: Loop st in each st (10 sts).

Rnd 8: Sc in each st (10 sts).

Fasten off and leave a 3-inch (7.5-cm) tail. Set aside.

Tail

Make a MR, then sc 8 into the MR (8 sts).

Rnds 1–2 (2 Rnds): Sc in each st (8 sts). Do not stuff.

Fasten off and leave a 12-inch (30.5-cm) tail for sewing.

Body

Ch 16.

Inc in the 2nd chain from hook, sc in the next 13 chs, and inc 2 times in the last ch. Turn your work clockwise 180 degrees, so that you can work along the opposite side of the chain. Then, sc in the next 13 chs, and inc in the last ch (34 sts).

Rnd 1: Inc in the first 2 sts, sc 13, inc in the next 4 sts, sc 13, inc in the last 2 sts (42 sts).

Rnd 2: Sc 2. Attach Leg 1 by placing your hook into the 6th st of the Leg and the next st of the Body. Sc the sts together. Sc the 5th st of the Leg and the next st of the Body. Sc the 4th st of the Leg and the next st of the Body together. Sc 12. Attach Leg 2 the same way the first Leg was attached. Sc 3. Attach the third Leg by placing your hook into the 1st st of the Leg and the next st of the Body. Sc the sts together. Sc the 10th st of the Leg and the next st of the Body together. Sc the 9th st of the Leg and the next st of the Body together. Sc 12. Attach Leg 4 the same way the previous Leg was attached. Sc in the last st (42 sts).

Rnd 3: Sc 2. Sc into the remaining 7 sts of Leg 1. Sc into the next 12 sts of the Body. Sc into the remaining 7 sts of Leg 2. Sc into the next 3 sts of the Body. Sc into the remaining 7 sts of Leg 3. Sc into the next 12 sts of the Body. Sc into the remaining 7 sts of Leg 4. Sc into the remaining st of the Body (58 sts).

Rnds 4–14 (11 Rnds): Sc in each st (58 sts).

Rnd 15: Sc 20, (dec, sc 3) 6 times, sc 8 (52 sts). Stuff the Legs.

Rnd 16: Sc in each st (52 sts). Start to stuff the Body.

Rnd 17: Sc 20, (dec, sc 2) 6 times, sc 8 (46 sts).

Rnd 18: Sc 39. Place a st marker in the 22nd st from the beginning of the round. Place your hook into the next st of the Body and the st marker st. Sl st the sts together. Repeat this process with the next st of the Body and the 21st st, the next st of the Body and the 20th st, the next st of the Body and the 19th st, the next st of the Body and the 18th st, and the next st of the Body and the 17th st. (You will now have 12 sts connected in the middle of the Body, and 2 openings, with 17 sts each.) Sc into the last st of the Body (40 sts). Remove the st marker. For more info on this section, refer to Blake the Boxer on page 49.

Rnd 19: Sc 16. Sc in the last st (17 sts).

Rnd 20: Sc in each st (17 sts).

Fasten off and leave a 12-inch (30.5-cm) tail for sewing.

To finish the Body, place your hook into the 23rd st of Rnd 18. Sc into the same st. Work into the remaining 16 sts by dec 8 times (9 sts). Finish stuffing the Body.

Rnd 21: (Dec, sc) 3 times (6 sts).

Fasten off and sew the hole closed.

Head

Make a MR and sc 8 into the MR (8 sts).

Rnd 1: Inc 8 times (16 sts).

Rnds 2–6 (5 Rnds): Sc in each st (16 sts). Attach safety eyes onto Rnd 6, 8 sts apart.

Rnd 7: (Inc, sc 3) 4 times (20 sts). Start to stuff the Head.

Rnd 8: Sc 9, inc 4 times, sc 7 (24 sts).

Rnd 9: Sc 9, (inc, sc) 4 times, sc 7 (28 sts).

Rnd 10: (Inc, sc 6) 4 times (32 sts).

Rnds 11–12 (2 Rnds): Sc in each st (32 sts). Continue to stuff the Head.

Rnd 13: Sc 17, loop st 6 times, sc 9 (32 sts).

Rnd 14: Sc in each st (32 sts).

Rnd 15: Sc 17, loop st 7 times, sc 8 (32 sts).

Rnd 16: Sc in each st (32 sts).

Rnd 17: Sc 18, loop st 6 times, sc 8 (32 sts).

Rnd 18: Sc in each st (32 sts).

Rnd 19: (Dec, sc 2) 8 times (24 sts).

Rnd 20: (Dec, sc) 8 times (16 sts). Finish stuffing the Head.

Rnd 21: Dec 8 times (8 sts).

Fasten off and sew the hole closed.

Ears (make 2)

Make a MR, then sc 8 into the MR (8 sts).

Rnd 1: Inc in each st (16 sts).

Rnd 2: Sc in each st (16 sts).

Rnd 3: Loop st in each st (16 sts).

Rnd 4: Sc in each st (16 sts).

Rnd 5: (Dec, sc 2) 4 times (12 sts).

Rnd 6: Loop st in each st (12 sts).

Rnd 7: Sc in each st (12 sts).

Rnd 8: Loop st in each st (12 sts).

Rnd 9: Sc in each st (12 sts).

Rnd 10: (Dec, sc) 4 times (8 sts).

Rnd 11: Sc in each st (8 sts).

Fasten off and leave a 12-inch (30.5-cm) tail for sewing.

Assembly

Sew each Ear onto Rnd 12 of the Head, 4 sts apart. Sew the Tail on the back of Rnd 20 of the Body. Sew the Head onto the neck of the Body. If you aren't using safety eyes, embroider a pair of eyes onto Rnd 6 of the Head, 8 sts apart. Finally, embroider a triangle-shaped nose 2 Rnds tall and 3 sts wide at its widest point on the Head.

Barns the Blue Heeler

This breed is gaining more attention due to a popular children's TV show. Its fur looks dark blue in the sun—hence its name. Try making a red heeler for a touch of personalization!

Skill Level

Intermediate

Size

Approx 6 inches (15 cm) long, 7 inches (18 cm) wide, and 10 inches (25.5 cm) tall

Yarn

Super chunky chenille yarn, Premier Yarns Parfait Chunky, 100% polyester, 131 yards (120 m), 3.5 oz (100 g)

- Gray (MC), 393 yds (360 m)
- Mustard (C1), 131 yds (120 m)
- Black (C2), 5 yds (5 m)

Hooks

US size H-8 (5mm)

Notions

Polyester fiberfill

Removable stitch marker used to mark the first stitch of the round (and other indicated stitches within a round)

Tapestry needle

Pair of 6-mm safety eyes (optional)

Gauge

20 sc x 18 rounds = 4 inches (10 cm)

Abbreviations

C1 = color 1

C2 = color 2

Ch(s) = chain(s)

Dec = decrease (crochet 2 sc together)

Flo = front loop only

Inc = increase (work 2 sc into one stitch)

MC = main color

MR = magic ring

Sc = single crochet

Sl st = slip stitch

St(s) = stitch(es)

Barns the Blue Heeler Pattern

Legs (make 4)

With C1, make a MR, then sc 8 into the MR (8 sts).

Rnd 1: Inc in each st (16 sts).

Rnds 2–3 (2 Rnds): Sc in each st (16 sts).

Rnd 4: Sc 4, dec 6 times (10 sts).

Rnds 5–7 (3 Rnds): Sc in each st (10 sts).

Sl st into the 1st st of Rnd 7.

Fasten off and leave a 3-inch (7.5-cm) tail. Set aside.

Tail

With C1, make a MR, then sc 8 into the MR (8 sts).

Rnds 1–4 (4 Rnds): Sc in each st (8 sts). Break C1.

Rnds 5–8 (4 Rnds): With C2, sc in each st (8 sts). Do not stuff.

Fasten off and leave a 12-inch (30.5-cm) tail for sewing.

Body

With C1, ch 16.

Inc in the 2nd chain from hook, sc in the next 13 chs, and inc 2 times in the last ch. Turn your work clockwise 180 degrees, so that you can work along the opposite side of the chain. Then, sc in the next 13 chs, and inc in the last ch (34 sts).

Rnd 1: Inc in the first 2 sts, sc 13, inc in the next 4 sts, sc 13, inc in the last 2 sts (42 sts).

Rnd 2: Sc 2. Attach Leg 1 by placing your hook into the 6th st of the Leg and the next st of the Body. Sc the sts together. Sc the 5th st of the Leg and the next st of the Body. Sc the 4th st of the Leg and the next st of the Body together. Sc 12. Attach Leg 2 the same way the first Leg was attached. Sc 3. Attach the third Leg by placing your hook into the 1st st of the Leg and the next st of the Body. Sc the sts together. Sc the 10th st of the Leg and the next st of the Body together. Sc the 9th st of the Leg and the next st of the Body together. Sc 12. Attach the last Leg the same way the previous Leg was attached. Sc in the last st (42 sts).

Rnd 3: Sc 2. Sc into the remaining 7 sts of Leg 1. Sc into the next 12 sts of the Body. Sc into the remaining 7 sts of Leg 2. Sc into the next 3 sts of the Body. Sc into the remaining 7 sts of Leg 3. Sc into the next 12 sts of the Body. Sc into the remaining 7 sts of Leg 4. Sc into the remaining st of the Body (58 sts).

Rnds 4–11 (8 Rnds): With C1, sc 12. With MC, sc 37. With C1, sc 9 (58 sts).

Rnds 12–13 (2 Rnds): With C1, sc 3. With MC, sc 3. With C1, sc 3. With MC, sc 49 (58 sts).

Rnd 14: With MC, sc 1. With C1, sc 2. With MC, sc 4. With C1, sc 2. With MC, sc 49 (58 sts). Break C1.

Rnd 15: With MC, sc 20, (dec, sc 3) 6 times, sc 8 (52 sts). Stuff the Legs. Break C1.

Rnd 16: With MC, sc in each st (52 sts). Start to stuff the Body.

Rnd 17: With MC, sc 20, (dec, sc 2) 6 times, sc 8 (46 sts). Break MC.

Rnd 18: With C1, sc 16. With C2, sc 23. Place a st marker in the 22nd st from the beginning of the round. Place your hook into the next st of the Body and the st marker st. Sl st the sts together. Repeat this process with the next st of the Body and the 21st st, the next st of the Body and the 20th st, the next st of the Body and the 19th st, the next st of the Body and the 18th st, and the next st of the Body and the 17th st. (You will now have 12 sts connected in the middle of the Body, and 2 openings, with 17 sts each.) With C1, sc into the last st of the Body (40 sts). Break C2. Remove the st marker. For more info on this section, refer to Blake the Boxer on page 49.

Rnd 19: With C1, sc 16. Sc in the last st (17 sts).

Rnd 20: Sc in each st (17 sts).

Fasten off and leave a 12-inch (30.5-cm) tail for sewing.

To finish the Body, with MC, place your hook into the 23rd st of Rnd 18. Sc into the same st. Work into the remaining 16 sts by dec 8 times (9 sts). Finish stuffing the Body.

Rnd 21: (Dec, sc) 3 times (6 sts).

Fasten off and sew the hole closed.

Head

With C1, ch 5.

Inc in the 2nd chain from hook, sc in the next 2 chs, and inc 2 times in the last ch. Turn your work clockwise 180 degrees, so that you can work along the opposite side of the chain. Then, sc in the next 2 chs, and inc in the last ch (12 sts).

Rnd 1: Inc 2, sc 2, inc 4 times, sc 2, inc 2 (20 sts).

Rnds 2–4 (3 Rnds): Sc in each st (20 sts).

Rnd 5: With C1, sc 15. With MC, sc 5 (20 sts).

Rnd 6: With MC, sc 9. With C2, sc, inc. With C1, inc 2 times. With C2, inc, sc. With MC, sc 5 (24 sts). Attach safety eyes to this Rnd, 8 sts apart.

Rnd 7: With MC, (inc, sc 3) 2 times, inc. With C2, sc 3, inc. With C1, sc 3. With C2, inc, sc 3, inc. With MC, sc 3 (30 sts). Break C1.

Rnd 8: With MC, sc 12. With C2, sc 6. With MC, sc 2. With C2, sc 7. With MC, sc 3 (30 sts).

Rnd 9: With MC, sc 12. With C2, sc 6. With MC, sc 3. With C2, sc 6. With MC, sc 3 (30 sts).

Rnd 10: With MC, sc 13. With C2, sc 6. With MC, sc 2. With C2, sc 6. With MC, sc 3 (30 sts).

Rnd 11: With MC, sc 14. With C2, sc 5. With MC, sc 3. With C2, sc 5. With MC, sc 3 (30 sts).

Rnd 12: With MC, sc 15. With C2, sc 4. With MC, sc 4. With C2, sc 4. With MC, sc 3 (30 sts). Break C2.

Rnds 13–15 (3 Rnds): With MC, sc in each st (30 sts).

Rnd 16: (Dec, sc 3) 6 times (24 sts). Stuff the Head.

Rnd 17: Sc in each st (24 sts).

Rnd 18: (Dec, sc 2) 6 times (18 sts).

Rnd 19: (Dec, sc) 6 times (12 sts).

Rnd 20: Dec 6 times (6 sts).

Fasten off and sew the hole closed.

Ears (make 2)

With C2, make a MR, then sc 6 into the MR (6 sts).

Rnd 1: (With C2, inc. With MC, sc 2) twice (8 sts).

Rnd 2: (With C2, sc 2. With MC, sc 2) twice (8 sts).

Rnd 3: (With MC, inc. With C2, sc 1. With MC, sc 2) twice (10 sts).

Rnd 4: (With MC, sc 2. With C2, sc 1. With MC, sc 2) twice (10 sts).

Rnd 5: (With MC, inc, sc. With C2, sc 1. With MC, sc 2) twice (12 sts).

Rnd 6: (With MC, inc, sc 2. With C2, sc 1. With MC, sc 2) twice (14 sts).

Rnd 7: (With MC, inc, sc 3. With C2, sc 1. With MC, sc 2) twice (16 sts).

Fasten off and leave a 12-inch (30.5-cm) tail for sewing.

Assembly

Sew each Ear onto Rnd 12 of the Head, 4 sts apart. Sew the Tail on the back of Rnd 20 of the Body. Sew the Head onto the neck of the Body. If you aren't using safety eyes, embroider a pair of eyes onto Rnd 6 of the Head, 8 sts apart. Finally, embroider a triangle-shaped nose 2 Rnds tall and 3 sts wide at its widest point on the Head.

The Cute Cats

Cats can be nonchalant at first glance . . . until you get to know them! In this chapter, I've included all types of cats—gingers, calicos, and even hairless cats—which means there's a guaranteed pattern that you can personalize to match your own! These plushies are designed so that you can create your own cat standing on all fours or sitting on two legs. Whether you're crocheting a stray cat that you brought indoors a few weeks ago or a tabby that has been in your household for years, this chapter is for you.

Sammy the Sphynx

Sphynx cats are very loving and energetic! Whether you're allergic to cat hair or you just love the feeling of their smooth skin, you'll enjoy making this pattern. Since there are many varieties of Sphynx, try creating one with a different color palette, such as black.

Skill Level

Intermediate

Size

Approx 6 inches (15 cm) long, 7 inches (18 cm) wide, and 10 inches (25.5 cm) tall

Yarn

Super chunky chenille yarn, Premier Yarns Parfait Chunky, 100% polyester, 131 yards (120 m), 3.5 oz (100 g)

- Cream (MC), 393 yds (360 m)
- Ballet Pink (C1), 20 yds (18 m)

Hooks

US size H-8 (5mm)

Notions

Polyester fiberfill

Removable stitch marker used to mark the first stitch of the round (and other indicated stitches within a round)

Tapestry needle

Pair of 6-mm safety eyes (optional)

Gauge

20 sc x 18 rounds = 4 inches (10 cm)

Abbreviations

C1 = color 1

Ch(s) = chain(s)

Dec = decrease (crochet 2 sc together)

Inc = increase (work 2 sc into one stitch)

MC = main color

MR = magic ring

Sc = single crochet

Sl st = slip stitch

St(s) = stitch(es)

Sammy the Sphynx Pattern

Legs (make 4)

With MC, make a MR, then sc 8 into the MR (8 sts).

Rnd 1: Inc in each st (16 sts).

Rnds 2–3 (2 Rnds): Sc in each st (16 sts).

Rnd 4: Sc 4, dec 6 times (10 sts).

Rnds 5–9 (5 Rnds): Sc in each st (10 sts).

Sl st into the 1st st of Rnd 9.

Fasten off and leave a 3-inch (7.5-cm) tail. Set aside.

Tail

With MC, make a MR, then sc 8 into the MR (8 sts).

Rnds 1–10 (10 Rnds): Sc in each st (8 sts).

Fasten off and leave a 12-inch (30.5-cm) tail for sewing.

Body

With C1, ch 16. Inc in the 2nd chain from hook, sc in the next 13 chs. Inc 2 times in the last ch. Rotate your work clockwise 180 degrees, so that you can work along the opposite side of the chain. Sc in the next 13 chs, and inc in the last ch (34 sts).

Rnd 1: Inc 2 times, sc 13, inc 4 times, sc 13, inc 2 times (42 sts).

Rnd 2: Sc 2. Attach Leg 1 by placing your hook into the 8th st of the Leg and the next st of the Body. Sc the sts together. Sc the 7th st of the Leg and the next st of the Body together. Sc the 6th st of the Leg and the next st of the Body together. Sc 12. Attach Leg 2 the same way the first Leg was attached. Sc 3. Attach Leg 3 by placing your hook into the 3rd st of the Leg and the next st of the Body. Sc the sts together. Sc the 2nd st of the Leg and the next st of the Body together. Sc the 1st st of the Leg and the next st of the Body together. Sc 12. Attach the last Leg the same way the previous Leg was attached. Sc in the last st (42 sts).

Rnd 3: With C1, sc into the first 2 sts of the Body. With MC, sc into the remaining 7 sts of Leg 1. Sc into the next 12 sts of the Body. Sc into the remaining 7 sts of Leg 2. Sc into the next 3 sts of the Body. Sc into the remaining 7 sts of Leg 3. Sc into the next 12 sts of the Body. Sc into the remaining 7 sts of Leg 4. With C1, sc into the remaining st of the Body (58 sts).

Rnd 4: With C1, sc 11. With MC, sc 38. With C1, sc 9 (58 sts).

Rnd 5: With C1, sc 12. With MC, sc 37. With C1, sc 9 (58 sts).

Rnd 6: With C1, sc 12. With MC, sc 38. With C1, sc 8 (58 sts).

Rnd 7: With C1, sc 10. With MC, sc 42. With C1, sc 6 (58 sts).

Rnd 8: With C1, sc 11. With MC, sc 41. With C1, sc 6 (58 sts).

Rnd 9: With C1, sc 11. With MC, sc 42. With C1, sc 5 (58 sts).

Rnd 10: With C1, sc 12. With MC, sc 41. With C1, sc 5 (58 sts).

Rnd 11: With C1, sc 12. With MC, sc 42. With C1, sc 4 (58 sts).

Rnd 12: With C1, sc 13. With MC, sc 41. With C1, sc 4 (58 sts).

Rnd 13: With C1, sc 13. With MC, sc 42. With C1, sc 3 (58 sts).

Rnd 14: With C1, sc 14. With MC, sc 41. With C1, sc 3 (58 sts).

Rnd 15: With C1, sc 14. With MC, sc 6, (dec, sc 3) 6 times, sc 6. With C1, sc 2 (52 sts).

Rnd 16: With C1, sc 15. With MC, sc 35. With C1, sc 2 (52 sts).

Rnd 17: With C1, sc 15. With MC, sc 5, (dec, sc 2) 6 times, sc 7. With C1, sc in last st (46 sts).

Rnd 18: With C1, sc 16. With MC, sc 23. Place a st marker in the 22nd st. Place your hook into the next st of the Body and the marked st. Sl st the sts together. Repeat this process with the next st of the Body and the 21st st, the next st of the Body and the 20th st, the next st of the Body and the 19th st, the next st of the Body and the 18th st, and the next st of the Body and the 17th st. (You will now have 12 sts connected in the middle of the Body, and 2 openings, with 17 sts each.) With C1, sc into the last st of the Body (40 sts). Break MC. Remove the st marker. For more info on this section, refer to Blake the Boxer on page 49.

Rnd 19: With C1, sc 16. Place your hook into the last st of the Rnd, and sc into the st (17 sts).

Rnd 20: Sc in each st (17 sts).

Fasten off and leave a 12-inch (30.5-cm) tail for sewing.

To finish the Body, place your hook into the 23rd st of Rnd 18. Sc into the same st. Work into the remaining 16 sts by dec 8 times (9 sts).

Rnd 21: (Dec, sc) 3 times (6 sts).

Fasten off and sew the hole closed.

Head

With MC, make a MR, then sc 6 into the MR (6 sts).

Rnd 1: Inc in each st (12 sts).

Rnd 2: Sc in each st (12 sts).

Rnd 3: Inc in the next 2 sts, sc 6, inc in the next 2 sts, sc 2 (16 sts).

Rnd 4: Inc in the next 4 sts, sc 5, inc in the next 4 sts, sc 3 (24 sts).

Rnd 5: Sc 9, inc in the next 4 sts, sc 11 (28 sts).

Rnd 6: Sc in each st (28 sts).

Rnd 7: Sc 9, (inc, sc) 4 times, sc 11 (32 sts). Attach safety eyes 8 sts apart.

Rnds 8–13 (6 Rnds): Sc in each st (32 sts).

Rnd 14: (Dec, sc 2) 8 times (24 sts). Stuff the Head.

Rnd 15: Sc in each st (24 sts).

Rnd 16: (Dec, sc 2) 6 times (18 sts).

Rnd 17: (Dec, sc) 6 times (12 sts).

Rnd 18: Dec 6 times (6 sts).

Fasten off and sew the hole closed.

Ears (make 2)

With MC, make a MR, then sc 6 into the MR (6 sts).

Rnd 1: Sc in each st (6 sts).

Rnd 2: With MC, sc 2. With C1, sc 2. With MC, sc 2 (6 sts).

Rnd 3: With MC, inc in the 1st st, sc. With C1, sc, inc in the next st. With MC, sc 2 (8 sts).

Rnd 4: With MC, sc 3. With C1, sc 3. With MC, sc 2 (8 sts).

Rnd 5: With MC, inc in the 1st st, sc 2. With C1, sc, inc in the next st, sc 2. With MC, sc in the last st (10 sts).

Rnd 6: With MC, inc in the 1st st, sc 3. With C1, sc, inc in the next st, sc 3. With MC, sc in the last st (12 sts).

Rnd 7: With MC, inc in the 1st st, sc 4. With C1, sc, inc in the next st, sc 5 (14 sts).

Fasten off and leave a 12-inch (30.5-cm) tail for sewing.

Assembly

Sew each Ear onto Rnd 12 of the Head, 4 sts apart. Sew the Tail on the back of Rnd 20 of the Body. Sew the Head onto the neck of the Body. If you aren't using the safety eyes, embroider a pair of eyes onto Rnd 7 of the Head, 8 sts apart. Finally, embroider a triangle-shaped nose 2 Rnds tall and 3 sts wide at its widest point on the Head.

Sarah the Siamese

This unique breed is known for their elongated body and their triangle-shaped head. In this pattern, I made the face fur look as distinct as possible. Make sure to double-check your rounds for stitches!

Skill Level

Beginner

Size

Approx 6 inches (15 cm) long, 7 inches (18 cm) wide, and 10 inches (25.5 cm) tall

Yarn

Super chunky chenille yarn, Premier Yarns Parfait Chunky, 100% polyester, 131 yards (120 m), 3.5 oz (100 g)

- White (MC), 393 yds (360 m)
- Black (C1), 131 yds (120 m)

Hooks

US size H-8 (5mm)

Notions

Polyester fiberfill

Removable stitch marker used to mark the first stitch of the round (and other indicated stitches within a round)

Tapestry needle

Pair of 6-mm safety eyes (optional)

Gauge

20 sc x 18 rounds = 4 inches (10 cm)

Abbreviations

C1 = color 1

Dec = decrease (crochet 2 sc together)

Flo = front loop only

Inc = increase (work 2 sc into one stitch)

MC = main color

MR = magic ring

Sc = single crochet

Sl st = slip stitch

St(s) = stitch(es)

Sarah the Siamese Pattern

Tail

With C1, make a MR, then sc 8 into the MR (8 sts).

Rnds 1–5 (5 Rnds): Sc in each st (8 sts).

Rnds 6–10 (5 Rnds): With MC, sc in each st (8 sts).

Fasten off and leave a 12-inch (30.5-cm) tail for sewing.

Front Legs (make 2)

With MC, make a MR, then sc 8 into the MR (8 sts).

Rnd 1: Inc in each st (16 sts).

Rnds 2–3 (2 Rnds): Sc in each st (16 sts).

Rnd 4: Sc 4, dec 6 times (10 sts).

Rnds 5–7 (3 Rnds): Sc in each st (10 sts).

Sl st into the 1st st of Rnd 7. Do not stuff.

Fasten off and leave a 3-inch (7.5-cm) tail. Set aside.

Back Legs (make 2)

Repeat Rnds 1–7 of the Front Leg. Stuff the Leg before you continue. (Only Rnds 1–7 will be stuffed.)

Rnd 8: Sc 5. In the flo, inc 5 times (15 sts).

Rnd 9: In the flo, inc 2. In both loops, sc 13 (17 sts).

Rnds 10–13 (4 Rnds): Sc in each st (17 sts).

Rnd 14: Dec 8, sc in last st (9 sts).

Fasten off and leave a 12-inch (30.5-cm) tail. Sew the hole closed. Set aside.

Body

With MC, make a MR, then sc 8 into the MR (8 sts).

Rnd 1: Inc in each st (16 sts).

Rnd 2: (Inc, sc) 8 times (24 sts).

Rnd 3: (Inc, sc 2) 8 times (32 sts).

Rnd 4: (Inc, sc 3) 8 times (40 sts).

Rnd 5: (Inc, sc 4) 8 times (48 sts).

Rnd 6: (Inc, sc 5) 8 times (56 sts).

Rnds 7–10 (4 Rnds): Sc in each st (56 sts).

Rnd 11: Sc 24, (dec, sc 2) 8 times (48 sts).

Rnd 12: Sc 8. Attach a Front Leg by placing your hook into the 5th st of the Leg and the next st of the Body. Sc the sts together. Sc the 4th st of the Leg and the next st of the Body. Sc the 3rd st of the Leg and the next st of the Body together. Sc 2. Attach the 2nd Front Leg the same way as the previous Leg. Sc 32 (48 sts).

Rnd 13: Sc into the next 8 sts of the Body. Sc into the remaining 7 sts of the Leg. Sc into the next 2 sts of the Body. Sc into the remaining 7 sts of the Leg. Sc into the remaining 32 sts of the Body (56 sts).

Rnds 14–15 (2 Rnds): Sc in each st (56 sts).

Rnd 16: Sc 29, (dec, sc 3) 5 times, dec in last 2 sts (50 sts).

Rnd 17: Sc 8, dec, sc 15, dec, sc 23 (48 sts).

Rnd 18: Sc 26, (sc 2, dec) 5 times, dec (42 sts).

Rnd 19: Sc 7, dec, sc 13, dec, sc 18 (40 sts).

Rnds 20–21 (2 Rnds): Sc in each st (40 sts).

Rnd 22: Sc 23, (sc, dec) 5 times, dec (34 sts).

Rnd 23: Sc 7, dec, sc 12, dec, sc 11 (32 sts).

Rnd 24: Sc in each st (32 sts).

Rnd 25: Sc 22, dec 5 (27 sts).

Rnd 26: Dec 3, sc 21 (24 sts).

Rnds 27–28 (2 Rnds): Sc in each st (24 sts).

Fasten off and leave a 12-inch (30.5-cm) tail for sewing.

Head

With C1, make a MR and sc 6 into the MR (6 sts).

Rnd 1: Inc 6 times (12 sts).

Rnd 2: Sc in each st (12 sts).

Rnd 3: Inc 2, sc 6, inc 2, sc 2 (16 sts).

Rnd 4: Inc 4, sc 6, inc 4, sc 2 (24 sts).

Rnd 5: Sc 9, inc 4, sc 11 (28 sts).

Rnd 6: With C1, sc 2. With MC, sc 6. With C1, sc 9. With MC, sc 6. With C1, sc 5 (28 sts).

Rnd 7: With C1, sc 2. With MC, sc 7, inc, sc. With C1, (inc, sc) 2 times. With MC, inc, sc 12 (32 sts). Attach safety eyes 8 sts apart.

Rnd 8: With MC, sc 14. With C1, sc 3. With MC, sc 15 (32 sts). Break C1.

Rnds 9–15 (7 Rnds): With MC, sc in each st (32 sts).

Rnd 16: (Dec, sc 2) 8 times (24 sts). Stuff the Head.

Rnd 17: Sc in each st (24 sts).

Rnd 18: (Dec, sc 2) 6 times (18 sts).

Rnd 19: (Dec, sc) 6 times (12 sts).

Rnd 20: Dec 6 times (6 sts).

Fasten off and sew the hole closed.

Ears (make 2)

With C1, make a MR and sc 6 into the MR (6 sts).

Rnd 1: Sc in each st (6 sts).

Rnd 2: (Inc, sc 2) 2 times (8 sts).

Rnd 3: Sc in each st (8 sts).

Rnd 4: (Inc, sc 3) 2 times (10 sts).

Rnd 5: (Inc, sc 4) 2 times (12 sts).

Rnd 6: (Inc, sc 2) 4 times (16 sts).

Rnds 7–10 (4 Rnds): Sc in each st (16 sts).

Fasten off and leave a 12-inch (30.5-cm) tail for sewing.

Assembly

Sew each Ear onto Rnd 12 of the Head, 4 sts apart. Sew each Back Leg onto Rnd 7 of the Body, next to the side of each Front Leg. Sew the Tail onto the back of Rnd 20 of the Body. Sew the Head onto the neck of the Body. If you aren't using safety eyes, embroider a pair of eyes onto Rnd 7 of the Head, 8 sts apart. Finally, embroider a triangle-shaped nose 2 Rnds tall and 3 sts wide at its widest point on the Head.

Tammy the Tabby

A basic cat? Maybe. But they're full of love! Tabby cats appear everywhere, so of course I had to include their iconic look in this collection. Don't be intimidated by all the stripes: I made sure to simplify the burden in this crochet rendition.

Skill Level

Intermediate

Size

Approx 6 inches (15 cm) long, 7 inches (18 cm) wide, and 10 inches (25.5 cm) tall

Yarn

Super chunky chenille yarn, Premier Yarns Parfait Chunky, 100% polyester, 131 yards (120 m), 3.5 oz (100 g)

- Toffee (MC), 393 yds (360 m)
- Espresso (C1), 131 yds (120 m)

Hooks

US size H-8 (5mm)

Notions

Polyester fiberfill

Removable stitch marker used to mark the first stitch of the round (and other indicated stitches within a round)

Tapestry needle

Pair of 6-mm safety eyes (optional)

Gauge

20 sc x 18 rounds = 4 inches (10 cm)

Abbreviations

C1 = color 1

Ch(s) = chain(s)

Dec = decrease (crochet 2 sc together)

Flo = front loop only

Inc = increase (work 2 sc into one stitch)

MC = main color

MR = magic ring

Sc = single crochet

Sl st = slip stitch

St(s) = stitch(es)

Tammy the Tabby Pattern

Tail

With MC, make a MR, then sc 8 into the MR (8 sts).

Rnds 1–10 (10 Rnds): Sc in each st (8 sts).

Fasten off and leave a 12-inch (30.5-cm) tail for sewing.

Front Legs (make 2)

With MC, make a MR, then sc 8 into the MR (8 sts).

Rnd 1: Inc in each st (16 sts).

Rnds 2–3 (2 Rnds): Sc in each st (16 sts).

Rnd 4: With C1, sc 4, dec 6 times (10 sts).

Rnds 5–6 (2 Rnds): Sc in each st (10 sts).

Rnd 7: With C1, sc in each st (10 sts).

Sl st into the 1st st of Rnd 7. Do not stuff.

Fasten off and leave a 3-inch (7.5-cm) tail. Set aside.

Back Legs (make 2)

Repeat Rnds 1–7 of the Front Leg. Stuff the Leg before you continue. (Only Rnds 1–7 will be stuffed.)

Rnd 8: Sc 5. Inc 5 times in the flo (15 sts).

Rnd 9: With C1, inc 2 times in the flo. In both loops, sc 13 (17 sts).

Rnds 10–11 (2 Rnds): With MC, sc in each st (17 sts).

Rnd 12: With C1, sc into each st (17 sts).

Rnd 13: With MC, sc in each st (17 sts).

Rnd 14: Dec 8, sc (9 sts).

Fasten off and leave a 12-inch (30.5-cm) tail for sewing. Sew the hole closed. Set aside.

Body

With MC, make a MR, then sc 8 into the MR (8 sts).

Rnd 1: Inc in each st (16 sts).

Rnd 2: (Inc, sc) 8 times (24 sts).

Rnd 3: (Inc, sc 2) 8 times (32 sts).

Rnd 4: (Inc, sc 3) 8 times (40 sts).

Rnd 5: (Inc, sc 4) 8 times (48 sts).

Rnd 6: (Inc, sc 5) 8 times (56 sts).

Rnds 7–8 (2 Rnds): With C1, sc in each st (56 sts).

Rnd 9: With MC, sc in each st (56 sts).

Rnd 10: With C1, sc in each st (56 sts).

Rnd 11: With MC, sc 24, (dec, sc 2) 8 times (48 sts).

Rnd 12: Sc 8. Attach a Front Leg by placing your hook into the 5th st of the Leg and the next st of the Body. Sc the sts together. Sc the 4th st of the Leg and the next st of the Body. Sc the 3rd st of the Leg and the next st of the Body together. Sc 2. Attach the 2nd Front Leg the same way as the previous Leg. Sc 32 (48 sts).

Rnd 13: Sc into the next 8 sts of the Body. Sc into the remaining 7 sts of the Leg. Sc into the next 2 sts of the Body. Sc into the remaining 7 sts of the Leg. Sc into the remaining 32 sts of the Body (56 sts).

Rnd 14: With C1, sc in each st (56 sts).

Rnd 15: Sc in each st (56 sts).

Rnd 16: With C1, sc 29, (dec, sc 3) 5 times, dec in last 2 sts (50 sts).

Rnd 17: Sc 8, dec, sc 15, dec, sc 23 (48 sts).

Rnd 18: With MC, sc 26, (sc 2, dec) 5 times, dec (42 sts).

Rnd 19: Sc 7, dec, sc 13, dec, sc 18 (40 sts).

Rnd 20: With C1, sc in each st (40 sts).

Rnd 21: With MC, sc in each st (40 sts).

Rnd 22: With C1, sc 23, (sc, dec) 5 times, dec (34 sts).

Rnd 23: Sc 7, dec, sc 12, dec, sc 11 (32 sts).

Rnd 24: With MC, sc in each st (32 sts).

Rnd 25: Sc 22, dec 5 (27 sts).

Rnd 26: With C1, dec 3, sc 21 (24 sts). Break C1.

Rnds 27–28 (2 Rnds): With MC, sc in each st (24 sts).

Fasten off and leave a 12-inch (30.5-cm) tail for sewing.

Head

With MC, make a MR and sc 6 into the MR (6 sts).

Rnd 1: Inc 6 times (12 sts).

Rnd 2: With MC, sc 3, (With C1, sc 1. With MC, sc 1) 2 times, with MC, sc 5 (12 sts).

Rnd 3: With MC, inc 2, sc 1. With C1, sc 1. With MC, sc 2. With C1, sc 1. With MC, sc, inc 2, sc 2 (16 sts).

Rnd 4: With MC, inc 4, sc 2. With C1, sc 1. With MC, sc 1. With C1, sc 1. With MC, sc, inc 4, sc 2 (24 sts).

Rnd 5: With MC, sc 10, inc 4, sc 10 (28 sts).

Rnd 6: With MC, sc 5. With C1, sc 1. With MC, sc 1. With C1, sc 1. With MC, sc 12. With C1, sc 1. With MC, sc 1. With C1, sc 1. With MC, sc 5 (28 sts).

Rnd 7: With MC, sc 5. With C1, sc 1. With MC, sc 1. With C1, sc 1. With MC, sc 2, inc, sc, inc. With C1, sc 1. With MC, inc. With C1, sc 1. With MC, sc 5. With C1, sc 1. With MC, sc 1. With C1, sc 1. With MC, sc 5 (32 sts). If using, attach safety eyes on this Rnd, 8 sts apart.

Rnd 8: With MC, sc 5. With C1, sc 1. With MC, sc 1. With C1, sc 1. With MC, sc 5. With C1, sc 1. With MC, sc 1. With C1, sc 1. With MC, sc 2. With C1, sc 1. With MC, sc 1. With C1, sc 1. With MC, sc 3. With C1, sc 1. With MC, sc 1. With C1, sc 1. With MC, sc 4 (32 sts).

Rnd 9: With MC, sc 5. With C1, sc 1. With MC, sc 1. With C1, sc 1. With MC, sc 8. With C1, sc 1. With MC, sc 1. With C1, sc 1. With MC, sc 6. With C1, sc 1. With MC, sc 1. With C1, sc 1. With MC, sc 4 (32 sts).

Rnd 10: With MC, sc 6. With C1, sc 2. With MC, sc 8. With C1, sc 1. With MC, sc 2. With C1, sc 1. With MC, sc 6. With C1, sc 2. With MC, sc 4 (32 sts).

Rnd 11: With MC, sc 7. With C1, sc 1. With MC, sc 9. With C1, sc 3. With MC, sc 7. With C1, sc 1. With MC, sc 4 (32 sts). Break C1.

Rnds 12–13 (2 Rnds): With MC, sc in each st (32 sts).

Rnd 14: (Dec, sc 2) 8 times (24 sts). Stuff the Head.

Rnd 15: Sc in each st (24 sts).

Rnd 16: (Dec, sc 2) 6 times (18 sts).

Rnd 17: (Dec, sc) 6 times (12 sts).

Rnd 18: Dec 6 times (6 sts).

Fasten off and sew the hole closed.

Ears (make 2)

With C1, make a MR, then sc 6 into the MR (6 sts).

Rnd 1: Sc in each st (6 sts).

Rnd 2: With C1, inc. With MC, sc 1. With C1, sc 1, inc, sc 2 (8 sts).

Rnd 3: With C1, sc 2. With MC, sc 2. With C1, sc 4 (8 sts).

Rnd 4: With C1, inc, sc. With MC, sc 2, inc. With C1, sc 3 (10 sts).

Rnds 5–6 (2 Rnds): With C1, inc, sc 2. With MC, sc 2, inc, sc 2. With C1, sc 2 (12 sts).

Fasten off and leave a 12-inch (30.5-cm) tail for sewing.

Assembly

Sew each Ear onto Rnd 12 of the Head, 4 sts apart. Sew each Back Leg onto Rnd 7 of the Body, beside each Front Leg. Sew the Tail onto the back of the Body on Rnd 20. Sew the Head onto the neck of the Body. If you aren't using safety eyes, embroider a pair of eyes onto Rnd 7 of the Head, 8 sts apart. Finally, embroider a triangle-shaped nose 2 Rnds tall and 3 sts wide at its widest point on the Head.

Gale the Ginger

As an iconic feline known for its "spicy" personality, this ginger cat is a must-have in our collection! Gingers look similar to Tabbies (page 83), but in this rendition I added more stripes, so be prepared for a challenge!

Skill Level

Intermediate

Size

Approx 6 inches (15 cm) long, 7 inches (18 cm) wide, and 10 inches (25.5 cm) tall

Yarn

Super chunky chenille yarn, Premier Yarns Parfait Chunky, 100% polyester, 131 yards (120 m), 3.5 oz (100 g)

- Orange (MC), 393 yds (360 m)
- Cream (C1), 131 yds (120 m)
- Mustard (C2), 5 yds (5 m)

Hooks

US size H-8 (5mm)

Notions

Polyester fiberfill

Removable stitch marker used to mark the first stitch of the round (and other indicated stitches within a round)

Tapestry needle

Pair of 6-mm safety eyes (optional)

Gauge

20 sc x 18 rounds = 4 inches (10 cm)

Abbreviations

C1 = color 1

C2 = color 2

Ch(s) = chain(s)

Dec = decrease (crochet 2 sc together)

Inc = increase (work 2 sc into one stitch)

MC = main color

MR = magic ring

Sc = single crochet

Sl st = slip stitch

St(s) = stitch(es)

Gale the Ginger Pattern

Legs (make 4)

With C1, make a MR, then sc 8 into the MR (8 sts).

Rnd 1: Inc in each st (16 sts).

Rnds 2–3 (2 Rnds): Sc in each st (16 sts). Break C1.

Rnd 4: With C2, sc 4, dec 6 times (10 sts).

Rnd 5: With MC, sc in each st (10 sts).

Rnds 6–7 (2 Rnds): With C2, sc in each st (10 sts).

Sl st into the 1st st of Rnd 7. Do not stuff.

Fasten off and leave a 3-inch (7.5-cm) tail. Set aside.

Tail

With C2 make a MR, then sc 8 into the MR (8 sts).

Rnds 1–2 (2 Rnds): Sc in each st (8 sts). Break C2.

Rnds 3–4 (2 Rnds): With C1, sc in each st (8 sts).

Rnds 5–6 (2 Rnds): With MC, sc in each st (8 sts).

Rnds 7–8 (2 Rnds): With C1, sc in each st (8 sts).

Rnds 9–10 (2 Rnds): With C1, sc in each st (8 sts). Do not stuff.

Fasten off and leave a 12-inch (30.5-cm) tail for sewing.

Body

With C1, ch 16.

Inc in the 2nd chain from hook, sc in the next 13 chs, and inc 2 times in the last ch. Turn your work clockwise 180 degrees, so that you can work along the opposite side of the chain. Then, sc in the next 13 chs, and inc in the last ch (34 sts).

Rnd 1: Inc in the first 2 sts, sc 13, inc in the next 4 sts, sc 13, inc in the last 2 sts (42 sts).

Rnd 2: Sc 2. Attach Leg 1 by placing your hook into the 6th st of the Leg and the next st of the Body. Sc the sts together. Sc the 5th st of the Leg and the next st of the Body. Sc the 4th st of the Leg and the next st of the Body together. Sc 12. Attach Leg 2 the same way the first Leg was attached. Sc 3. Attach the third Leg by placing your hook into the 1st st of the Leg and the next st of the Body. Sc the sts together. Sc the 10th st of the Leg and the next st of the Body together. Sc the 9th st of the Leg and the next st of the Body together. Sc 12. Attach the last Leg the same way the previous Leg was attached. Sc in the last st (42 sts).

Rnd 3: Sc 2. Sc into the remaining 7 sts of Leg 1. Sc into the next 12 sts of the Body. Sc into the remaining 7 sts of Leg 2. Sc into the next 3 sts of the Body. Sc into the remaining 7 sts of Leg 3. Sc into the next 12 sts of the Body. Sc into the remaining 7 sts of Leg 4. Sc into the remaining st of the Body (58 sts).

Rnd 4: With C1, sc 3. (With MC, sc 3. With C2, sc 2. With MC, sc 2. With C2, sc 1) 6 times. With MC, sc 3. With C2, sc 2. With C1, sc 2 (58 sts).

Rnds 5–6 (2 Rnds): With C1, sc 4. (With MC, sc 3. With C2, sc 2. With MC, sc 2. With C2, sc 1) 6 times. With MC, sc 3. With C2, sc 2. With C1, sc 1 (58 sts).

Rnds 7–8 (2 Rnds): With C1, sc 5. (With MC, sc 3. With C2, sc 2. With MC, sc 2. With C2, sc 1) 6 times. With MC, sc 3. With C2, sc 2 (58 sts).

Rnd 9: With C1, sc 6. (With MC, sc 3. With C2, sc 2. With MC, sc 2. With C2, sc 1) 6 times. With MC, sc 3. With C2, sc 1 (58 sts).

Rnd 10: With C2, sc 1. With C1, sc 5. (With MC, sc 3. With C2, sc 2. With MC, sc 2. With C2, sc 1) 6 times. With MC, sc 3. With C2, sc 1 (58 sts).

Rnd 11: With C1, sc 1. With C1, sc 6. (With MC, sc 3. With C2, sc 2. With MC, sc 2. With C2, sc 1) 6 times. With MC, sc 3 (58 sts).

Rnd 12: With C2, sc 2. With C1, sc 5. (With MC, sc 3. With C2, sc 2. With MC, sc 2. With C2, sc 1) 6 times. With MC, sc 3 (58 sts).

Rnd 13: With C2, sc 2. With C1, sc 6. (With MC, sc 3. With C2, sc 2. With MC, sc 2. With C2, sc 1) 6 times. With MC, sc 2 (58 sts).

Rnd 14: With MC, sc 1. With C2, sc 2. With C1, sc 5. (With MC, sc 3. With C2, sc 2. With MC, sc 2. With C2, sc 1) 6 times. With MC, sc 2 (58 sts).

Rnd 15: With MC, sc 1. With C2, sc 2. With C1, sc 6. With MC, sc 11, (dec, sc 3) 6 times, sc 8 (52 sts). Stuff the Legs. Break C2.

Rnd 16: With MC, sc 4. With C1, sc 5. With MC, sc 43 (52 sts). Start to stuff the Body.

Rnd 17: With MC, sc 4. With C1, sc 6. With MC, sc 10, (dec, sc 2) 6 times, sc 8 (46 sts).

Rnd 18: With MC, sc 5. With C1, sc 5. With MC, sc 29. Place a st marker in the 22nd st from the beginning of the round. Place your hook into the next st of the Body and the marked st. Sl st the sts together. Repeat this process with the next st of the Body and the 21st st, the next st of the Body and the 20th st, the next st of the Body and the 19th st, the next st of the Body and the 18th st, and the next st of the Body and the 17th st. (You will now have 12 sts connected in the middle of the Body, and 2 openings, with 17 sts each.) With MC, sc into the last st of the Body (40 sts). Break C1. Remove the st marker. For more info on this section, refer to Blake the Boxer on page 49.

Rnd 19: With MC, sc 17 (17 sts).

Rnd 20: Sc in each st (17 sts).

Fasten off and leave a 12-inch (30.5-cm) tail for sewing.

To finish the Body, with MC, place your hook into the 23rd st of Rnd 18. Sc into the same st. Work into the remaining 16 sts by dec 8 times (9 sts). Finish stuffing the Body.

Rnd 21: (Dec, sc) 3 times (6 sts).

Fasten off and sew the hole closed.

Head

With C1, make a MR and sc 6 into the MR (6 sts).

Rnd 1: Inc 6 times (12 sts).

Rnd 2: With MC, sc 3. (With C2, sc 1. With MC, sc 1) 2 times, with MC, sc 5 (12 sts).

Rnd 3: With MC, inc 2, sc 1. With C2, sc 1. With MC, sc 2. With C2, sc 1. With MC, sc, inc 2, sc 2 (16 sts).

Rnd 4: With MC, inc 4, sc 2. With C2, sc 1. With MC, sc 1. With C2, sc 1. With MC, sc, inc 4, sc 2 (24 sts).

Rnd 5: With MC, sc 10, inc 4, sc 10 (28 sts).

Rnd 6: With MC, sc 5. With C2, sc 1. With MC, sc 1. With C2, sc 1. With MC, sc 12. With C2, sc 1. With MC, sc 1. With C2, sc 1. With MC, sc 5 (28 sts).

Rnd 7: With MC, sc 5. With C2, sc 1. With MC, sc 1. With C2, sc 1. With MC, sc 2, inc, sc, inc. With C2, sc 1. With MC, inc. With C2, sc 1. With MC, sc 5. With C2, sc 1. With MC, sc 1. With C2, sc 1. With MC, sc 4 (31 sts). Attach safety eyes 8 sts apart.

Rnd 8: With MC, sc 5. With C2, sc 1. With MC, sc 1. With C2, sc 1. With MC, sc 5. With C2, sc 1. With MC, sc 1. With C2, sc 1. With MC, sc 2. With C2, sc 1. With MC, sc 1. With C2, sc 1. With MC, sc 3. With C2, sc 1. With MC, sc 1. With C2, sc 1. With MC, sc 4 (31 sts).

Rnd 9: With MC, sc 5. With C2, sc 1. With MC, sc 1. With C2, sc 1. With MC, sc 8. With C2, sc 1. With MC, sc 1. With C2, sc 1. With MC, sc 6. With C2, sc 1. With MC, sc 1. With C2, sc 1. With MC, sc 3 (31 sts).

Rnd 10: With MC, sc 6. With C2, sc 2. With MC, sc 8. With C2, sc 1. With MC, sc 2. With C2, sc 1. With MC, sc 6. With C2, sc 2. With MC, sc 3 (31 sts).

Rnd 11: With MC, sc 7. With C2, sc 1. With MC, sc 9. With C2, sc 3. With MC, sc 7. With C2, sc 1. With MC, sc 3 (31 sts). Break C2.

Rnds 12–13 (2 Rnds): With MC, sc in each st (31 sts).

Rnd 14: (Dec, sc 2) 7 times, sc 3 (24 sts). Stuff the Head.

Rnd 15: Sc in each st (24 sts).

Rnd 16: (Dec, sc 2) 6 times (18 sts).

Rnd 17: (Dec, sc) 6 times (12 sts).

Rnd 18: Dec 6 times (6 sts).

Fasten off and sew the hole closed.

Ears (make 2)

With C2, make a MR and sc 6 into the MR (6 sts).

Rnd 1: Sc in each st (6 sts).

Rnd 2: (Inc, sc 2) 2 times (8 sts).

Rnd 3: Sc in each st (8 sts).

Rnd 4: (Inc, sc 3) 2 times (10 sts).

Rnd 5: (Inc, sc 4) 2 times (12 sts). Break C2.

Rnd 6: With MC, (inc, sc 5) 2 times (16 sts). Do not stuff.

Rnds 7–10 (4 Rnds): Sc in each st (16 sts).

Fasten off and leave a 12-inch (30.5-cm) tail for sewing.

Assembly

Sew each Ear onto Rnd 12 of the Head, 4 sts apart. Sew the Tail on the back of Rnd 20 of the Body. Sew the Head onto the neck of the Body. If you aren't using safety eyes, embroider a pair of eyes onto Rnd 7 of the Head, 8 sts apart. Finally, embroider a triangle-shaped nose 2 Rnds tall and 3 sts wide at its widest point on the Head.

Benny the Black Bombay

Benny is a cat that blends in with the night sky. Black Bombays may seem easy to crochet, but the color of the yarn adds a challenge. For this pattern, make sure to work in brighter rooms or under a bright lamp so you're able to see the darker-colored stitches!

Skill Level

Intermediate

Size

Approx 6 inches (15 cm) long, 7 inches (18 cm) wide, and 10 inches (25.5 cm) tall

Yarn

Super chunky chenille yarn, Premier Yarns Parfait Chunky, 100% polyester, 131 yards (120 m), 3.5 oz (100 g)

- Black (MC), 393 yds (360 m)

Hooks

US size H-8 (5mm)

Notions

Polyester fiberfill

Removable stitch marker used to mark the first stitch of the round (and other indicated stitches within a round)

Tapestry needle

Pair of 6-mm safety eyes (optional)

Gauge

20 sc x 18 rounds = 4 inches (10 cm)

Abbreviations

Ch(s) = chain(s)

Dec = decrease (crochet 2 sc together)

Flo = front loop only

Inc = increase (work 2 sc into one stitch)

MC = main color

MR = magic ring

Sc = single crochet

Sl st = slip stitch

St(s) = stitch(es)

Benny the Black Bombay Pattern

Tail

With MC, make a MR, then sc 8 into the MR (8 sts).

Rnds 1–10 (10 Rnds): Sc in each st (8 sts).

Fasten off and leave a 12-inch (30.5-cm) tail for sewing.

Front Legs (make 2)

With MC, make a MR, then sc 8 into the MR (8 sts).

Rnd 1: Inc in each st (16 sts).

Rnds 2–3 (2 Rnds): Sc in each st (16 sts).

Rnd 4: Sc 4, dec 6 times (10 sts).

Rnds 5–7 (3 Rnds): Sc in each st (10 sts).

Sl st into the 1st st of Rnd 7. Do not stuff.

Fasten off and leave a 3-inch (7.5-cm) tail. Set aside.

Back Legs (make 2)

Repeat Rnds 1–7 of the Front Leg. Stuff the Leg before you continue. (Only Rnds 1–7 will be stuffed.)

Rnd 8: Sc 5. Inc 5 times in the flo (15 sts).

Rnd 9: Inc 2 times in the flo. In both loops, sc 13 (17 sts).

Rnds 10–13 (4 Rnds): Sc in each st (17 sts).

Rnd 14: Dec 8, sc (9 sts).

Fasten off and leave a 12-inch (30.5-cm) tail for sewing. Sew the hole closed. Set aside.

Body

With MC, make a MR, then sc 8 into the MR (8 sts).

Rnd 1: Inc in each st (16 sts).

Rnd 2: (Inc, sc) 8 times (24 sts).

Rnd 3: (Inc, sc 2) 8 times (32 sts).

Rnd 4: (Inc, sc 3) 8 times (40 sts).

Rnd 5: (Inc, sc 4) 8 times (48 sts).

Rnd 6: (Inc, sc 5) 8 times (56 sts).

Rnds 7–10 (4 Rnds): Sc in each st (56 sts).

Rnd 11: Sc 24, (dec, sc 2) 8 times (48 sts).

Rnd 12: Sc 8. Attach a Front Leg by placing your hook into the 5th st of the Leg and the next st of the Body. Sc the sts together. Sc the 4th st of the Leg and the next st of the Body. Sc the 3rd st of the Leg and the next st of the Body together. Sc 2. Attach the 2nd Front Leg the same way as the previous Leg. Sc 32 (48 sts).

Rnd 13: Sc into the next 8 sts of the Body. Sc into the remaining 7 sts of the Leg. Sc into the next 2 sts of the Body. Sc into the remaining 7 sts of the Leg. Sc into the remaining 32 sts of the Body (56 sts).

Rnds 14–15 (2 Rnds): Sc in each st (56 sts).

Rnd 16: Sc 29, (dec, sc 3) 5 times, dec in last 2 sts (50 sts).

Rnd 17: Sc 8, dec, sc 15, dec, sc 23 (48 sts).

Rnd 18: Sc 26, (sc 2, dec) 5 times, dec (42 sts).

Rnd 19: Sc 7, dec, sc 13, dec, sc 18 (40 sts).

Rnds 20–21 (2 Rnds): Sc in each st (40 sts).

Rnd 22: Sc 23, (sc, dec) 5 times, dec (34 sts).

Rnd 23: Sc 7, dec, sc 12, dec, sc 11 (32 sts).

Rnd 24: Sc in each st (32 sts).

Rnd 25: Sc 22, dec 5 (27 sts).

Rnd 26: Dec 3, sc 21 (24 sts).

Rnds 27–28 (2 Rnds): Sc in each st (24 sts).

Fasten off and leave a 12-inch (30.5-cm) tail for sewing.

Head

With MC, make a MR and sc 6 into the MR (6 sts).

Rnd 1: Inc 6 times (12 sts).

Rnd 2: Sc in each st (12 sts).

Rnd 3: Inc 2, sc 6, inc 2, sc 2 (16 sts).

Rnd 4: Inc 4, sc 5, inc 4, sc 2 (24 sts).

Rnd 5: Sc 9, inc 4, sc 11 (28 sts).

Rnd 6: Sc in each st (28 sts).

Rnd 7: Sc 9, (inc, sc) 4 times, sc 11 (32 sts). Attach safety eyes 8 sts apart.

Rnds 8–13 (6 Rnds): Sc in each st (32 sts).

Rnd 14: (Dec, sc 2) 8 times (24 sts). Stuff the Head.

Rnd 15: Sc in each st (24 sts).

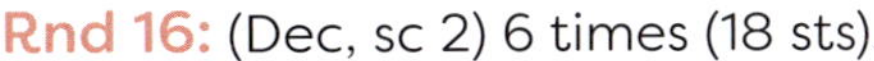

Rnd 16: (Dec, sc 2) 6 times (18 sts).

Rnd 17: (Dec, sc) 6 times (12 sts).

Rnd 18: Dec 6 times (6 sts).

Fasten off and sew the hole closed.

Ears (make 2)

With MC, make a MR and sc 6 into the MR (6 sts).

Rnd 1: Sc in each st (6 sts).

Rnd 2: (Inc, sc 2) 2 times (8 sts).

Rnd 3: Sc in each st (8 sts).

Rnd 4: (Inc, sc 3) 2 times (10 sts).

Rnd 5: (Inc, sc 4) 2 times (12 sts).

Rnd 6: (Inc, sc 2) 4 times (16 sts).

Rnds 7–10 (4 Rnds): Sc in each st (16 sts).

Fasten off and leave a 12-inch (30.5-cm) tail for sewing.

Assembly

Sew each Ear onto Rnd 12 of the Head, 4 sts apart. Sew each Back Leg onto Rnd 7 of the Body, beside each Front Leg. Sew the Tail onto the back of the Body on Rnd 20. Sew the Head onto the neck of the Body. If you aren't using safety eyes, embroider a pair of eyes onto Rnd 7 of the Head, 8 sts apart. Finally, embroider a triangle-shaped nose 2 Rnds tall and 3 sts wide at its widest point on the Head.

Sophia the Snowshoe

Did you know that snowshoes are a mix of Siamese and American shorthair breeds? This pattern is fun to work because of the tri-coloring involved. Although this breed is rare, you'll soon be able to have your own right in your home.

Skill Level

Intermediate

Size

Approx 6 inches (15 cm) long, 7 inches (18 cm) wide, and 10 inches (25.5 cm) tall

Yarn

Super chunky chenille yarn, Premier Yarns Parfait Chunky, 100% polyester, 131 yards (120 m), 3.5 oz (100 g)

- Cream (MC), 393 yds (360 m)
- Gray (C1), 131 yds (120 m)
- Black (C2), 131 yds (120 m)

Hooks

US size H-8 (5mm)

Notions

Polyester fiberfill

Removable stitch marker used to mark the first stitch of the round (and other indicated stitches within a round)

Tapestry needle

Pair of 6-mm safety eyes (optional)

Gauge

20 sc x 18 rounds = 4 inches (10 cm)

Abbreviations

C1 = color 1

C2 = color 2

Ch(s) = chain(s)

Dec = decrease (crochet 2 sc together)

Inc = increase (work 2 sc into one stitch)

MC = main color

MR = magic ring

Sc = single crochet

Sl st = slip stitch

St(s) = stitch(es)

Sophia the Snowshoe Pattern

Legs (make 4)

With MC, make a MR, then sc 8 into the MR (8 sts).

Rnd 1: Inc in each st (16 sts).

Rnds 2–3 (2 Rnds): Sc in each st (16 sts).

Rnd 4: Sc 4, dec 6 times (10 sts). Break MC.

Rnds 5–7 (3 Rnds): With C2, sc in each st (10 sts). Sl st into the 1st st of Rnd 7.

Fasten off and leave a 3-inch (7.5-cm) tail. Set aside.

Tail

With C2, make a MR, then sc 8 into the MR (8 sts).

Rnds 1–10 (10 Rnds): Sc in each st (8 sts).

Fasten off and leave a 12-inch (30.5-cm) tail for sewing.

Body

With MC, ch 16.

Inc in the 2nd chain from hook, sc in the next 13 chs, and inc 2 times in the last ch. Turn your work clockwise 180 degrees, so that you can work along the opposite side of the chain. Then, sc in the next 13 chs, and inc in the last ch (34 sts).

Rnd 1: Inc in the first 2 sts, sc 13, inc in the next 4 sts, sc 13, inc in the last 2 sts (42 sts).

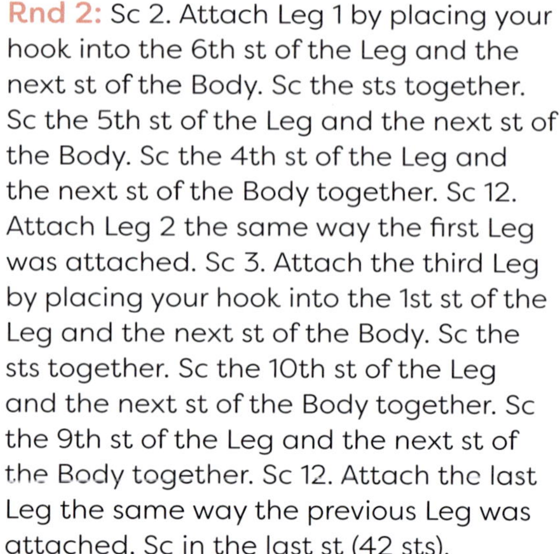

Rnd 2: Sc 2. Attach Leg 1 by placing your hook into the 6th st of the Leg and the next st of the Body. Sc the sts together. Sc the 5th st of the Leg and the next st of the Body. Sc the 4th st of the Leg and the next st of the Body together. Sc 12. Attach Leg 2 the same way the first Leg was attached. Sc 3. Attach the third Leg by placing your hook into the 1st st of the Leg and the next st of the Body. Sc the sts together. Sc the 10th st of the Leg and the next st of the Body together. Sc the 9th st of the Leg and the next st of the Body together. Sc 12. Attach the last Leg the same way the previous Leg was attached. Sc in the last st (42 sts).

Rnd 3: Sc 2. Sc into the remaining 7 sts of Leg 1. Sc into the next 12 sts of the Body. Sc into the remaining 7 sts of Leg 2. Sc into the next 3 sts of the Body. Sc into the remaining 7 sts of Leg 3. Sc into the next 12 sts of the Body. Sc into the remaining 7 sts of Leg 4. Sc into the remaining st of the Body (58 sts).

Rnd 4: With MC, sc 11. With C1, sc 38. With MC, sc 9 (58 sts).

Rnd 5: With MC, sc 12. With C1, sc 37. With MC, sc 9 (58 sts).

Rnd 6: With MC, sc 12. With C1, sc 38. With MC, sc 8 (58 sts).

Rnd 7: With MC, sc 10. With C1, sc 42. With MC, sc 6 (58 sts).

Rnd 8: With MC, sc 11. With C1, sc 41. With MC, sc 6 (58 sts).

Rnd 9: With MC, sc 11. With C1, sc 42. With MC, sc 5 (58 sts).

Rnd 10: With MC, sc 12. With C1, sc 41. With MC, sc 5 (58 sts).

Rnd 11: With MC, sc 12. With C1, sc 42. With MC, sc 4 (58 sts).

Rnd 12: With MC, sc 13. With C1, sc 41. With MC, sc 4 (58 sts).

Rnd 13: With MC, sc 13. With C1, sc 42. With MC, sc 3 (58 sts).

Rnd 14: With MC, sc 14. With C1, sc 41. With MC, sc 3 (58 sts).

Rnd 15: With MC, sc 14. With C1, sc 6, (dec, sc 3) 6 times, sc 6. With MC, sc 2 (52 sts). Stuff the Legs.

Rnd 16: With MC, sc 15. With C1, sc 35. With MC, sc 2 (52 sts). Start to stuff the Body.

Rnd 17: With MC, sc 15. With C1, sc 5, (dec, sc 2) 6 times, sc 7. With MC, sc in the last st (46 sts).

Rnd 18: With MC, sc 16. With C1, sc 23. Place a st marker in the 22nd st from the beginning of the round. Place your hook into the next st of the Body and the marked st. Sl st the sts together. Repeat this process with the next st of the Body and the 21st st, the next st of the Body and the 20th st, the next st of the Body and the 19th st, the next st of the Body and the 18th st, and the next st of the Body and the 17th st. (You will now have 12 sts connected in the middle of the Body, and 2 openings, with 17 sts each.) With C1, sc into the last st of the Body (40 sts). Break C1. Remove the st marker. For more info on this section, refer to Blake the Boxer on page 49.

Rnd 19: With C1, sc 17 (17 sts).

Rnd 20: Sc in each st (17 sts).

Fasten off and leave a 12-inch (30.5-cm) tail for sewing.

To finish the Body, with MC, place your hook into the 23rd st of Rnd 18. Sc into the same st. Work into the remaining 16 sts by dec 8 times (9 sts). Finish stuffing the Body.

Rnd 21: (Dec, sc) 3 times (6 sts).

Fasten off and sew the hole closed.

Head

With MC, make a MR and sc 6 into the MR (6 sts).

Rnd 1: Inc 6 times (12 sts).

Rnd 2: Inc 2, sc 6, inc 2, sc 2 (16 sts).

Rnd 3: With MC, inc 2. With C2, inc 2, sc. With MC, sc 3. With C2, sc 2, inc 2. With MC, inc 2, sc 2 (24 sts).

Rnd 4: With MC, sc 4. With C2, sc 5, inc. With MC, inc 2. With C2, inc, sc 6. With MC, sc 5 (28 sts).

Rnd 5: With MC, sc 5. With C2, sc 6, inc 2. With MC, inc 1. With C2, inc, sc 8. With MC, sc 5 (32 sts).

Rnd 6: With MC, sc 5. With C2, sc 11. With MC, sc 1. With C2, sc 10. With MC, sc 5 (32 sts). Place safety eyes 7 sts apart on this Rnd.

Rnd 7: With MC, sc 6. With C2, sc 6, (inc, sc) 4 times, sc 7. With MC, sc 5 (36 sts).

Rnd 8: With MC, sc 9. With C1, sc 20. With MC, sc 7 (36 sts).

Rnd 9: With MC, sc 12. With C1, sc 15. With MC, sc 9 (36 sts). Break C1.

Rnds 10–13 (4 Rnds): With MC, sc in each st (36 sts).

Rnd 14: (Dec, sc 2) 9 times (27 sts). Stuff the Head.

Rnd 15: Sc in each st (27 sts).

Rnd 16: (Dec, sc) 9 times (18 sts).

Rnd 17: (Dec, sc) 6 times (12 sts).

Rnd 18: Dec 6 times (6 sts).

Fasten off and sew the hole closed.

Ears (make 2)

With C2, make a MR, then sc 6 into the MR (6 sts).

Rnd 1: Sc in each st (6 sts).

Rnd 2: With C2, inc. With C1, sc 1. With C2, sc 1, inc, sc 2 (8 sts).

Rnd 3: With C2, sc 2. With C1, sc 2. With C2, sc 4 (8 sts).

Rnd 4: With C2, inc, sc. With C1, sc 2, inc. With C2, sc 3 (10 sts).

Rnd 5: With C2, inc, sc 2. With C1, sc 2, inc, sc 2. With C2, sc 2 (12 sts).

Fasten off and leave a 12-inch (30.5-cm) tail for sewing.

Assembly

Sew each Ear onto Rnd 12 of the Head, 4 sts apart. Sew the Tail on the back of Rnd 20 of the Body. Sew the Head onto the neck of the Body. If you aren't using safety eyes, embroider a pair of eyes onto Rnd 6 of the Head, 8 sts apart. Finally, embroider a triangle-shaped nose 2 Rnds tall and 3 sts wide at its widest point on the Head.

Bernie the Burmese

This cat breed is high in attention—and love! Burmese cats are known for having a cat-like appearance but a dog-like personality. Work this pattern in a brightly lit room so you're able to see the darker stitches more easily!

Skill Level

Intermediate

Size

Approx 6 inches (15 cm) long, 7 inches (18 cm) wide, and 10 inches (25.5 cm) tall

Yarn

Super chunky chenille yarn, Premier Yarns Parfait Chunky, 100% polyester, 131 yards (120 m), 3.5 oz (100 g)

- Toffee (MC), 393 yds (360 m)
- Espresso (C1), 131 yds (120 m)

Hooks

US size H-8 (5mm)

Notions

Polyester fiberfill

Removable stitch marker used to mark the 1st stitch of the round (and other indicated stitches within a round)

Tapestry needle

Pair of 6-mm safety eyes (optional)

Gauge

20 sc x 18 rounds = 4 inches (10 cm)

Abbreviations

C1 = color 1

Ch(s) = chain(s)

Dec = decrease (crochet 2 sc together)

Inc = increase (work 2 sc into one stitch)

MC = main color

MR = magic ring

Sc = single crochet

Sl st = slip stitch

St(s) = stitch(es)

Bernie the Burmese Pattern

Legs (make 4)

With C1, make a MR, then sc 8 into the MR (8 sts).

Rnd 1: Inc in each st (16 sts).

Rnds 2–3 (2 Rnds): Sc in each st (16 sts).

Rnd 4: Sc 4, dec 6 times (10 sts).

Rnds 5–7 (3 Rnds): Sc in each st (10 sts).

Sl st into the 1st st of Rnd 7.

Fasten off and leave a 3-inch (7.5-cm) tail. Set aside.

Tail

With C1, make a MR, then sc 8 into the MR (8 sts).

Rnds 1–4 (4 Rnds): Sc in each st (8 sts).

Rnds 5–8 (4 Rnds): With C1, sc in each st (8 sts). Do not stuff.

Fasten off and leave a 12-inch (30.5-cm) tail for sewing.

Body

With MC, ch 16.

Inc in the 2nd chain from hook, sc in the next 13 chs, and inc 2 times in the last ch. Turn your work clockwise 180 degrees, so that you can work along the opposite side of the chain. Then, sc in the next 13 chs, and inc in the last ch (34 sts).

Rnd 1: Inc in the first 2 sts, sc 13, inc in the next 4 sts, sc 13, inc in the last 2 sts (42 sts).

Rnd 2: Sc 2. Attach Leg 1 by placing your hook into the 6th st of the Leg and the next st of the Body. Sc the sts together. Sc the 5th st of the Leg and the next st of the Body. Sc the 4th st of the Leg and the next st of the Body together. Sc 12. Attach Leg 2 the same way the first Leg was attached. Sc 3. Attach the third Leg by placing your hook into the 1st st of the Leg and the next st of the Body. Sc the sts together. Sc the 10th st of the Leg and the next st of the Body together. Sc the 9th st of the Leg and the next st of the Body together. Sc 12. Attach the last Leg the same way the previous Leg was attached. Sc in the last st (42 sts).

Rnd 3: Sc 2. Sc into the remaining 7 sts of Leg 1. Sc into the next 12 sts of the Body. Sc into the remaining 7 sts of Leg 2. Sc into the next 3 sts of the Body. Sc into the remaining 7 sts of Leg 3. Sc into the next 12 sts of the Body. Sc into the remaining 7 sts of Leg 4. Sc into the remaining st of the Body (58 sts).

Rnd 4: With MC, sc 11. With C1, sc 38. With MC, sc 9 (58 sts).

Rnd 5: With MC, sc 12. With C1, sc 37. With MC, sc 9 (58 sts).

Rnd 6: With MC, sc 12. With C1, sc 38. With MC, sc 8 (58 sts).

Rnd 7: With MC, sc 10. With C1, sc 42. With MC, sc 6 (58 sts).

Rnd 8: With MC, sc 11. With C1, sc 41. With MC, sc 6 (58 sts).

Rnd 9: With MC, sc 11. With C1, sc 42. With MC, sc 5 (58 sts).

Rnd 10: With MC, sc 12. With C1, sc 41. With MC, sc 5 (58 sts).

Rnd 11: With MC, sc 12. With C1, sc 42. With MC, sc 4 (58 sts).

Rnd 12: With MC, sc 13. With C1, sc 41. With MC, sc 4 (58 sts).

Rnd 13: With MC, sc 13. With C1, sc 42. With MC, sc 3 (58 sts).

Rnd 14: With MC, sc 14. With C1, sc 41. With MC, sc 3 (58 sts).

Rnd 15: With MC, sc 14. With C1, sc 6, (dec, sc 3) 6 times, sc 6. With MC, sc 2 (52 sts). Stuff the Legs.

Rnd 16: With MC, sc 15. With C1, sc 35. With MC, sc 2 (52 sts). Start to stuff the Body.

Rnd 17: With MC, sc 15. With C1, sc 5, (dec, sc 2) 6 times, sc 7. With MC, sc in the last st (46 sts).

Rnd 18: With MC, sc 16. With C1, sc 23. Place a st marker in the 22nd st from the beginning of the round. Place your hook into the next st of the Body and the st marker st. Sl st the sts together. Repeat this process with the next st of the Body and the 21st st, the next st of the Body and the 20th st, the next st of the Body and the 19th st, the next st of the Body and the 18th st, and the next st of the Body and the 17th st. (You will now have 12 sts connected in the middle of the Body, and 2 openings, with 17 sts each.) With C1, sc into the last st of the Body (40 sts). Break C1. Remove the st marker. For more info on this section, refer to Blake the Boxer on page 49.

Rnd 19: With MC, sc 16. Sc in the last st (17 sts).

Rnd 20: Sc in each st (17 sts).

Fasten off and leave a 12-inch (30.5-cm) tail for sewing.

To finish the Body, with MC, place your hook into the 23rd st of Rnd 18. Sc into the same st. Work into the remaining 16 sts by dec 8 times (9 sts). Finish stuffing the Body.

Rnd 21: (Dec, sc) 3 times (6 sts).

Fasten off and sew the hole closed.

Head

With C1, make a MR and sc 6 into the MR (6 sts).

Rnd 1: Inc 6 times (12 sts).

Rnd 2: Sc in each st (12 sts).

Rnd 3: Inc 2, sc 6, inc 2, sc 2 (16 sts).

Rnd 4: Inc 4, sc 6, inc 4. With MC, sc 2 (24 sts).

Rnd 5: With MC, sc 2. With C1, sc 7, inc 4, sc 8. With MC, sc 3 (28 sts).

Rnd 6: With MC, sc 3. With C1, sc 7. With MC, sc 2. With C1, sc 4. With MC, sc 2. With C1, sc 7. With MC, sc 3 (28 sts).

Rnd 7: With MC, sc 4. With C1, sc 5, inc. With MC, sc, inc. With C1, (sc, inc) 2 times. With MC, sc 3. With C1, sc 6. With MC, sc 3 (32 sts). If using, attach safety eyes on this Rnd, 8 sts apart.

Rnd 8: With MC, sc 6. With C1, sc 4. With MC, sc 6. With C1, sc 3. With MC, sc 6. With C1, sc 3. With MC, sc 4 (32 sts).

Rnd 9: With MC, sc 17. With C1, sc 2. With MC, sc 13 (32 sts). Break C1.

Rnds 10–15 (6 Rnds): With MC, sc in each st (32 sts).

Rnd 16: (Dec, sc 2) 8 times (24 sts). Stuff the Head.

Rnd 17: Sc in each st (24 sts).

Rnd 19: (Dec, sc 2) 6 times (18 sts).

Rnd 20: (Dec, sc) 6 times (12 sts).

Rnd 21: Dec 6 times (6 sts).

Fasten off and sew the hole closed.

Ears (make 2)

With C1, make a MR, then sc 6 into the MR (6 sts).

Rnd 1: Sc in each st (6 sts).

Rnd 2: With C1, inc. With MC, sc 1. With C1, sc 1, inc, sc 2 (8 sts).

Rnd 3: With C1, sc 2. With MC, sc 2. With C1, sc 4 (8 sts).

Rnd 4: With C1, inc, sc. With MC, sc 2, inc. With C1, sc 3 (10 sts).

Rnd 5: With C1, inc, sc 2. With MC, sc 2, inc, sc 2. With C1, sc 2 (12 sts).

Fasten off and leave a 12-inch (30.5-cm) tail for sewing.

Assembly

Sew each Ear onto Rnd 12 of the Head, 4 sts apart. Sew the Tail on the back of Rnd 20 of the Body. Sew the Head onto the neck of the Body. If you aren't using safety eyes, embroider a pair of eyes onto Rnd 6 of the Head, 8 sts apart. Finally, embroider a triangle-shaped nose 2 Rnds tall and 3 sts wide at its widest point on the Head.

Carrie the Calico

Although calicos are not a breed, their unique coat color deserves a spot in the cat collection! Creating calicos can be a challenge due to their tri-coloring, so make sure to keep your yarn separate so it doesn't tangle.

Skill Level

Intermediate

Size

Approx 6 inches (15 cm) long, 7 inches (18 cm) wide, and 10 inches (25.5 cm) tall

Yarn

Super chunky chenille yarn, Premier Yarns Parfait Chunky, 100% polyester, 131 yards (120 m), 3.5 oz (100 g)

- Mustard (MC), 393 yds (360 m)
- Cream (C1), 131 yds (120 m)
- Black (C2), 131 yds (120 m)

Hooks

US size H-8 (5mm)

Notions

Polyester fiberfill

Removable stitch marker used to mark the first stitch of the round (and other indicated stitches within a round)

Tapestry needle

Pair of 6-mm safety eyes (optional)

Gauge

20 sc x 18 rounds = 4 inches (10 cm)

Abbreviations

C1 = color 1

C2 = color 2

Ch(s) = chain(s)

Dec = decrease (crochet 2 sc together)

Inc = increase (work 2 sc into one stitch)

MC = main color

MR = magic ring

Sc = single crochet

Sl st = slip stitch

St(s) = stitch(es)

Carrie the Calico Pattern

Legs (make 4)

With C1, make a MR, then sc 8 into the MR (8 sts).

Rnd 1: Inc in each st (16 sts).

Rnds 2–3 (2 Rnds): Sc in each st (16 sts).

Rnd 4: Sc 4, dec 6 times (10 sts). Break C1.

Rnds 5–7 (3 Rnds): With MC, sc in each st (10 sts).

Sl st into the 1st st of Rnd 7.

Fasten off and leave a 3-inch (7.5-cm) tail. Set aside.

Tail

With C2, make a MR, then sc 8 into the MR (8 sts).

Rnds 1–5 (5 Rnds): Sc in each st (8 sts). Break C2.

Rnds 6–10 (5 Rnds): With MC, sc in each st (8 sts).

Fasten off and leave a 12-inch (30.5-cm) tail for sewing.

Body

With C1, ch 16.

Inc in the 2nd chain from hook, sc in the next 13 chs, and inc 2 times in the last ch. Turn your work clockwise 180 degrees, so that you can work along the opposite side of the chain. Then, sc in the next 13 chs, and inc in the last ch (34 sts).

Rnd 1: Inc in the first 2 sts, sc 13, inc in the next 4 sts, sc 13, inc in the last 2 sts (42 sts).

Rnd 2: Sc 2. Attach Leg 1 by placing your hook into the 6th st of the Leg and the next st of the Body. Sc the sts together. Sc the 5th st of the Leg and the next st of the Body. Sc the 4th st of the Leg and the next st of the Body together. Sc 12. Attach Leg 2 the same way the first Leg was attached. Sc 3. Attach the third Leg by placing your hook into the 1st st of the Leg and the next st of the Body. Sc the sts together. Sc the 10th st of the Leg and the next st of the Body together. Sc the 9th st of the Leg and the next st of the Body together. Sc 12. Attach the last Leg the same way the previous Leg was attached. Sc in the last st (42 sts).

Rnd 3: Sc 2. With MC, sc into the remaining 7 sts of Leg 1. Sc into the next 12 sts of the Body. Sc into the remaining 7 sts of Leg 2. Sc into the next 3 sts of the Body. Sc into the remaining 7 sts of Leg 3. Sc into the next 12 sts of the Body. Sc into the remaining 7 sts of Leg 4. Sc into the remaining st of the Body (58 sts).

Rnd 4: With MC, sc 10. With C2, sc 3. With MC, sc 3. With C2, sc 4. With MC, sc 19. With C2, sc 4. With MC, sc 2. With C2, sc 3. With MC, sc 10 (58 sts).

Rnd 5: With MC, sc 11. With C2, sc 3. With MC, sc 3. With C2, sc 4. With MC, sc 18. With C2, sc 4. With MC, sc 2. With C2, sc 3. With MC, sc 10 (58 sts).

Rnd 6: With MC, sc 12. With C2, sc 3. With MC, sc 3. With C2, sc 4. With MC, sc 17. With C2, sc 4. With MC, sc 2. With C2, sc 3. With MC, sc 10 (58 sts).

Rnd 7: With MC, sc 13. With C2, sc 3. With MC, sc 3. With C2, sc 4. With MC, sc 16. With C2, sc 4. With MC, sc 2. With C2, sc 3. With MC, sc 10 (58 sts).

Rnd 8: With MC, sc 14. With C2, sc 3. With MC, sc 3. With C2, sc 4. With MC, sc 15. With C2, sc 4. With MC, sc 2. With C2, sc 3. With MC, sc 10 (58 sts).

Rnd 9: With MC, sc 15. With C2, sc 3. With MC, sc 3. With C2, sc 4. With MC, sc 14. With C2, sc 4. With MC, sc 2. With C2, sc 3. With MC, sc 10 (58 sts).

Rnd 10: With MC, sc 2. With C1, sc 3. With MC, sc 11. With C2, sc 3. With MC, sc 3. With C2, sc 4. With MC, sc 13. With C2, sc 4. With MC, sc 2. With C2, sc 3. With MC, sc 10 (58 sts).

Rnd 11: With MC, sc 2. With C1, sc 4. With MC, sc 11. With C2, sc 3. With MC, sc 3. With C2, sc 4. With MC, sc 12. With C2, sc 4. With MC, sc 2. With C2, sc 3. With MC, sc 10 (58 sts).

Rnd 12: With MC, sc 2. With C1, sc 5. With MC, sc 12. With C2, sc 2. With MC, sc 4. With C2, sc 3. With MC, sc 12. With C2, sc 3. With MC, sc 3. With C2, sc 2. With MC, sc 10 (58 sts).

Rnd 13: With MC, sc 2. With C1, sc 6. With MC, sc 12. With C2, sc 1. With MC, sc 5. With C2, sc 2. With MC, sc 13. With C2, sc 2. With MC, sc 4. With C2, sc 1. With MC, sc 10 (58 sts).

Rnd 14: With MC, sc 2. With C1, sc 7. With MC, sc 18. With C2, sc 1. With MC, sc 14. With C2, sc 1. With MC, sc 15 (58 sts). Break C2.

Rnd 15: With MC, sc 2. With C1, sc 8. With MC, sc 10, (dec, sc 3) 6 times, sc 8 (52 sts). Stuff the Legs.

Rnd 16: With MC, sc 2. With C1, sc 9. With MC, sc 41 (52 sts). Start to stuff the Body.

Rnd 17: With MC, sc 2. With C1, sc 8. With MC, sc 10, (dec, sc 2) 6 times, sc 7. With MC, sc in the last st (46 sts).

Rnd 18: With MC, sc 2. With C1, sc 9. With MC, sc 28. Place a st marker in the 22nd st from the beginning of the round. Place your hook into the next st of the Body and the marked st. Sl st the sts together. Repeat this process with the next st of the Body and the 21st st, the next st of the Body and the 20th st, the next st of the Body and the 19th st, the next st of the Body and the 18th st, and the next st of the Body and the 17th st. (You will now have 12 sts connected in the middle of the Body, and 2 openings, with 17 sts each.) With C1, sc into the last st of the Body (40 sts). Break MC. Remove the st marker. For more info on this section, refer to Blake the Boxer on page 49.

Rnd 19: With C1, sc 16. Sc in the last st (17 sts).

Rnd 20: Sc in each st (17 sts).

Fasten off and leave a 12-inch (30.5-cm) tail for sewing.

To finish the Body, with MC, place your hook into the 23rd st of Rnd 18. Sc into the same st. Work into the remaining 16 sts by dec 8 times (9 sts). Finish stuffing the Body.

Rnd 21: (Dec, sc) 3 times (6 sts).

Fasten off and sew the hole closed.

Head

With C1, make a MR and sc 6 into the MR (6 sts).

Rnd 1: Inc 6 times (12 sts).

Rnd 2: Inc 2, sc 6, inc 2, sc 2 (16 sts).

Rnd 3: With C1, inc 2. With C2, inc 2, sc. With C1, sc 3. With MC, sc 2, inc 2. With C1, inc 2, sc 2 (24 sts).

Rnd 4: With C1, sc 4. With C2, sc 5, inc. With C1, inc 2. With MC, inc, sc 6. With C1, sc 5 (28 sts).

Rnd 5: With C1, sc 5. With C2, sc 6, inc 2. With C1, inc. With C2, inc. With MC, sc 8. With C1, sc 5 (32 sts).

Rnd 6: With C1, sc 5. With C2, sc 11. With C1, sc 1. With C2, sc 2. With MC, sc 8. With C1, sc 5 (32 sts). Attach safety eyes to this Rnd, 8 sts apart.

Rnd 7: With C1, sc 6. With C2, sc 6, (inc, sc) 4 times. With MC, sc 7. With C1, sc 5 (36 sts).

Rnd 8: With C1, sc 9. With C2, sc 16. With MC, sc 4. With C1, sc 7 (36 sts). Break MC.

Rnd 9: With C1, sc 12. With C2, sc 15. With C1, sc 9 (36 sts). Break C2.

Rnds 10–15 (6 Rnds): With C1, sc in each st (36 sts).

Rnd 16: (Dec, sc 2) 9 times (27 sts). Stuff the Head.

Rnd 17: Sc in each st (27 sts).

Rnd 19: (Dec, sc) 9 times (18 sts).

Rnd 19: (Dec, sc) 6 times (12 sts).

Rnd 20: Dec 6 times (6 sts).

Fasten off and sew the hole closed.

Ears (make 2)

With C2, make a MR, then sc 6 into the MR (6 sts).

Rnd 1: Sc in each st (6 sts).

Rnd 2: With C2, inc. With C1, sc 1. With C2, sc 1, inc, sc 2 (8 sts).

Rnd 3: With C2, sc 2. With C1, sc 2. With C2, sc 4 (8 sts).

Rnd 4: With C2, inc, sc. With C1, sc 2, inc. With C2, sc 3 (10 sts).

Rnd 5: With C2, inc, sc 2. With C1, sc 2, inc, sc 2. With C2, sc 2 (12 sts).

Fasten off and leave a 12-inch (30.5-cm) tail for sewing.

Assembly

Sew each Ear onto Rnd 12 of the Head, 4 sts apart. Sew the Tail on the back of Rnd 20 of the Body. Sew the Head onto the neck of the Body. If you aren't using safety eyes, embroider a pair of eyes onto Rnd 6 of the Head, 8 sts apart. Finally, embroider a triangle-shaped nose 2 Rnds tall and 3 sts wide at its widest point on the Head.

Penelope the Persian

Persians—which are famous for their long hair—are one of the oldest cat breeds in the world. If you prefer to make a fluffier version, add more loop stitches!

Skill Level

Advanced

Size

Approx 6 inches (15 cm) long, 7 inches (18 cm) wide, and 10 inches (25.5 cm) tall

Yarn

Super chunky chenille yarn, Premier Yarns Parfait Chunky, 100% polyester, 131 yards (120 m), 3.5 oz (100 g)

- White (MC), 393 yds (360 m)
- Ballet Pink (C1), 131 yds (120 m)

Hooks

US size H-8 (5mm)

Notions

Polyester fiberfill

Removable stitch marker used to mark the first stitch of the round (and other indicated stitches within a round)

Tapestry needle

Pair of 6-mm safety eyes (optional)

Gauge

20 sc x 18 rounds = 4 inches (10 cm)

Abbreviations

C1 = color 1

Ch(s) = chain(s)

Dec = decrease (crochet 2 sc together)

Flo = front loop only

Inc = increase (work 2 sc into one stitch)

MC = main color

MR = magic ring

Sc = single crochet

Sl st = slip stitch

St(s) = stitch(es)

Special Stitches

Loop Stitch (loop st): Place your hook into the next st, yarn over, and draw a loop. Remove the loop from your hook, place your hook into the front loop of the stitch, yarn over, and draw a loop. Yarn over, and pull through the remaining two loops on your hook. See page 8 for a photo tutorial of this stitch.

Penelope the Persian Pattern

Tail

With MC, make a MR, then sc 8 into the MR (8 sts).

Rnds 1–10 (10 Rnds): Sc in each st (8 sts).

Fasten off and leave a 12-inch (30.5-cm) tail for sewing.

Front Legs (make 2)

With MC, make a MR, then sc 8 into the MR (8 sts).

Rnd 1: Inc in each st (16 sts).

Rnd 2: Loop st in each st (16 sts).

Rnd 3: Sc in each st (16 sts).

Rnd 4: Sc 4, dec 6 times (10 sts).

Rnd 5: Loop st in each st (10 sts).

Rnd 6: Sc in each st (10 sts).

Rnd 7: Loop st in each st (10 sts).

Sl st into the 1st st of Rnd 7. Do not stuff.

Fasten off and leave a 3-inch (7.5-cm) tail. Set aside.

Back Legs (make 2)

Repeat Rnds 1–7 of the Front Leg. Stuff the Leg before you continue. (Only Rnds 1–7 will be stuffed.)

Rnd 8: Sc 5. Inc 5 times in the flo (15 sts).

Rnd 9: Inc 2 times in the flo. In both loops, loop st in the remaining 13 sts (17 sts).

Rnd 10: Sc in each st (17 sts).

Rnd 11: Loop st in each st (17 sts).

Rnd 12: Sc in each st (17 sts).

Rnd 13: Loop st in each st (17 sts).

Rnd 14: Dec 8, sc in last st (9 sts).

Fasten off and leave a 12-inch (30.5-cm) tail. Sew the hole closed. Set aside.

Body

With MC, make a MR, then sc 8 into the MR (8 sts).

Rnd 1: Inc in each st (16 sts).

Rnd 2: (Inc, sc) 8 times (24 sts).

Rnd 3: (Inc, sc 2) 8 times (32 sts).

Rnd 4: (Inc, sc 2, loop st) 8 times (40 sts).

Rnd 5: (Inc, sc 4) 8 times (48 sts).

Rnd 6: (Inc, loop st 5 times) 8 times (56 sts).

Rnd 7: Sc in each st (56 sts).

Rnd 8: Loop st in each st (56 sts).

Rnd 9: Sc in each st (56 sts).

Rnd 10: Loop st in each st (56 sts).

Rnd 11: Sc 24, (dec, sc 2) 8 times (48 sts).

Rnd 12: Sc 8. Attach a Front Leg by placing your hook into the 5th st of the Leg and the next st of the Body. Sc the sts together. Sc the 4th st of the Leg and the next st of the Body. Sc the 3rd st of the Leg and the next st of the Body together. Sc 2. Attach the 2nd Front Leg the same way as the previous Leg. Sc 32 (48 sts).

Rnd 13: Sc into the next 8 sts of the Body. Sc into the remaining 7 sts of the Leg. Sc into the next 2 sts of the Body. Sc into the remaining 7 sts of the Leg. Sc into the remaining 32 sts of the Body (56 sts). Start to stuff the Legs.

Rnd 14: Loop st in each st (56 sts).

Rnd 15: Sc in each st (56 sts).

Rnd 16: Loop st 29 times, (dec, sc 3) 5 times, dec in last 2 sts (50 sts).

Rnd 17: Sc 8, dec, sc 15, dec, sc 23 (48 sts). Finish stuffing the Legs. Start stuffing the Body.

Rnd 18: Loop st 26 times, (sc 2, dec) 5 times, dec (42 sts).

Rnd 19: Sc 7, dec, sc 13, dec, sc 18 (40 sts).

Rnd 20: Loop st in each st (40 sts). Continue to stuff the Body.

Rnd 21: Sc in each st (40 sts).

Rnd 22: Loop st 23 times, (sc, dec) 5 times, dec (34 sts).

Rnd 23: Sc 7, dec, sc 12, dec, sc 11 (32 sts).

Rnd 24: Loop st in each st (32 sts).

Rnd 25: Sc 22, dec 5 (27 sts).

Rnd 26: Dec 3, loop st 21 times (24 sts). Finish stuffing the Body.

Rnd 27: Loop st in each st (24 sts).

Rnd 28: Sc in each st (24 sts).

Fasten off and leave a 12-inch (30.5-cm) tail for sewing.

Head

With MC, make a MR and sc 6 into the MR (6 sts).

Rnd 1: Inc 6 times (12 sts).

Rnd 2: Sc in each st (12 sts).

Rnd 3: Inc 2, loop st 6 times, inc 2, sc 2 (16 sts).

Rnd 4: Inc 4, sc 6, inc 4, sc 2 (24 sts).

Rnd 5: Loop st 9 times, inc 4, loop st 11 times (28 sts).

Rnd 6: Sc in each st (28 sts).

Rnd 7: Loop st 9 times, (inc, sc) 4 times, loop st 11 times (32 sts). Attach safety eyes onto this Rnd, 8 sts apart.

Rnd 8: Sc in each st (32 sts).

Rnd 9: Loop st in each st (32 sts).

Rnd 10: Sc in each st (32 sts).

Rnd 11: Loop st in each st (32 sts).

Rnd 12: Sc in each st (32 sts).

Rnd 13: Loop st in each st (32 sts).

Rnd 14: (Dec, sc 2) 8 times (24 sts). Stuff the Head.

Rnd 15: Loop st in each st (24 sts).

Rnd 16: (Dec, sc 2) 6 times (18 sts).

Rnd 17: (Dec, sc) 6 times (12 sts).

Rnd 18: Dec 6 times (6 sts).

Fasten off and sew the hole closed.

Ears (make 2)

With MC, make a MR, then sc 6 into the MR (6 sts).

Rnd 1: Sc in each st (6 sts).

Rnd 2: With MC, inc. With C1, sc 1. With MC, sc 1, inc, sc 2 (8 sts).

Rnd 3: With MC, sc 2. With C1, sc 2. With MC, sc 4 (8 sts).

Rnd 4: With MC, inc, sc. With C1, sc 2, inc. With MC, sc 3 (10 sts).

Rnd 5: With MC, inc, sc 2. With C1, sc 2, inc, sc 2. With MC, sc 2 (12 sts).

Fasten off and leave a 12-inch (30.5-cm) tail for sewing.

Assembly

Sew each Ear onto Rnd 12 of the Head, 4 sts apart. Sew each Back Leg onto Rnd 7 of the Body, beside each Front Leg. Sew the Tail onto the back of the Body on Rnd 20. Sew the Head onto the neck of the Body. If you aren't using safety eyes, embroider a pair of eyes onto Rnd 7 of the Head, 8 sts apart. Finally, embroider a triangle-shaped nose 2 Rnds tall and 3 sts wide at its widest point on the Head.

Hallie the Hairless Cat

This pattern is for the feline lovers who are allergic to feline hair! Although their beauty is in the eye of the beholder, they are such iconic cats, I had to add them to this collection.

Skill Level

Intermediate

Size

Approx 6 inches (15 cm) long, 7 inches (18 cm) wide, and 10 inches (25.5 cm) tall

Yarn

Super chunky chenille yarn, Premier Yarns Parfait Chunky, 100% polyester, 131 yards (120 m), 3.5 oz (100 g)

- Shell (MC), 393 yds (360 m)
- Light Gray (C1), 131 yds (120 m)
- Pink (C2), 5 yds (5 m)

Hooks

US size H-8 (5mm)

Notions

Polyester fiberfill

Removable stitch marker used to mark the first stitch of the round (and other indicated stitches within a round)

Tapestry needle

Pair of 6-mm safety eyes (optional)

Gauge

20 sc x 18 rounds = 4 inches (10 cm)

Abbreviations

C1 = color 1

C2 = color 2

Ch(s) = chain(s)

Dec = decrease (crochet 2 sc together)

Inc = increase (work 2 sc into one stitch)

MC = main color

MR = magic ring

Sc = single crochet

Sl st = slip stitch

St(s) = stitch(es)

Hallie the Hairless Cat Pattern

Legs (make 4)

With MC, make a MR, then sc 8 into the MR (8 sts).

Rnd 1: Inc in each st (16 sts).

Rnds 2–3 (2 Rnds): Sc in each st (16 sts).

Rnd 4: Sc 4, dec 6 times (10 sts).

Rnds 5–7 (3 Rnds): Sc in each st (10 sts).

Sl st into the 1st st of Rnd 7.

Fasten off and leave a 3-inch (7.5-cm) tail. Set aside.

Tail

With MC, make a MR, then sc 8 into the MR (8 sts).

Rnds 1–10 (10 Rnds): Sc in each st (8 sts).

Fasten off and leave a 12-inch (30.5-cm) tail for sewing.

Body

With MC, ch 16.

Inc in the 2nd chain from hook, sc in the next 13 chs, and inc 2 times in the last ch. Turn your work clockwise 180 degrees, so that you can work along the opposite side of the chain. Then, sc in the next 13 chs, and inc in the last ch (34 sts).

Rnd 1: Inc in the first 2 sts, sc 13, inc in the next 4 sts, sc 13, inc in the last 2 sts (42 sts).

Rnd 2: Sc 2. Attach Leg 1 by placing your hook into the 6th st of the Leg and the next st of the Body. Sc the sts together. Sc the 5th st of the Leg and the next st of the Body. Sc the 4th st of the Leg and the next st of the Body together. Sc 12. Attach Leg 2 the same way the first Leg was attached. Sc 3. Attach the third Leg by placing your hook into the 1st st of the Leg and the next st of the Body. Sc the sts together. Sc the 10th st of the Leg and the next st of the Body together. Sc the 9th st of the Leg and the next st of the Body together. Sc 12. Attach the last Leg the same way the previous Leg was attached. Sc in the last st (42 sts).

Rnd 3: Sc 2. Sc into the remaining 7 sts of Leg 1. Sc into the next 12 sts of the Body. Sc into the remaining 7 sts of Leg 2. Sc into the next 3 sts of the Body. Sc into the remaining 7 sts of Leg 3. Sc into the next 12 sts of the Body. Sc into the remaining 7 sts of Leg 4. Sc into the remaining st of the Body (58 sts).

Rnd 4: With MC, sc 11. With C1, sc 38. With MC, sc 9 (58 sts).

Rnd 5: With MC, sc 12. With C1, sc 37. With MC, sc 9 (58 sts).

Rnd 6: With MC, sc 12. With C1, sc 38. With MC, sc 8 (58 sts).

Rnd 7: With MC, sc 10. With C1, sc 42. With MC, sc 6 (58 sts).

Rnd 8: With MC, sc 11. With C1, sc 41. With MC, sc 6 (58 sts).

Rnd 9: With MC, sc 11. With C1, sc 42. With MC, sc 5 (58 sts).

Rnd 10: With MC, sc 12. With C1, sc 41. With MC, sc 5 (58 sts).

Rnd 11: With MC, sc 12. With C1, sc 42. With MC, sc 4 (58 sts).

Rnd 12: With MC, sc 13. With C1, sc 41. With MC, sc 4 (58 sts).

Rnd 13: With MC, sc 13. With C1, sc 42. With MC, sc 3 (58 sts).

Rnd 14: With MC, sc 14. With C1, sc 41. With MC, sc 3 (58 sts).

Rnd 15: With MC, sc 14. With C1, sc 6, (dec, sc 3) 6 times, sc 6. With MC, sc 2 (52 sts). Stuff the Legs.

Rnd 16: With MC, sc 15. With C1, sc 35. With MC, sc 2 (52 sts). Start to stuff the Body.

Rnd 17: With MC, sc 15. With C1, sc 5, (dec, sc 2) 6 times, sc 7. With MC, sc in the last st (46 sts).

Rnd 18: With MC, sc 16. With C1, sc 23. Place a st marker in the 22nd st from the beginning of the round. Place your hook into the next st of the Body and the marked st. Sl st the sts together. Repeat this process with the next st of the Body and the 21st st, the next st of the Body and the 20th st, the next st of the Body and the 19th st, the next st of the Body and the 18th st, and the next st of the Body and the 17th st. (You will now have 12 sts connected in the middle of the Body, and 2 openings, with 17 sts each.) With C1, sc into the last st of the Body (40 sts). Break MC. Remove the st marker. For more info on this section, refer to Blake the Boxer on page 49.

Rnd 19: With C1, sc 16. Sc in the last st (17 sts).

Rnd 20: Sc in each st (17 sts).

Fasten off and leave a 12-inch (30.5-cm) tail for sewing.

To finish the Body, with C1, place your hook into the 23rd st of Rnd 18. Sc into the same st. Work into the remaining 16 sts by dec 8 times (9 sts). Finish stuffing the Body.

Rnd 21: (Dec, sc) 3 times (6 sts).

Fasten off and sew the hole closed.

Head

With MC, make a MR, then sc 8 into the MR (8 sts).

Rnd 1: Inc in each st (16 sts).

Rnds 2–4 (3 Rnds): Sc in each st (16 sts).

Rnd 5: Sc 7, inc 3 times, sc 2, inc 3 times, sc in the last st (22 sts).

Rnd 6: Sc 7, (inc, sc) 3 times, sc 2, (inc, sc) 3 times, sc in last st (28 sts). Place safety eyes on this Rnd, 7 sts apart.

Rnd 7: Sc in each st (28 sts). Start to stuff the Head.

Rnd 8: Sc 7, inc, (sc 2, inc) 2 times, sc 4, (inc, sc 2) 3 times, sc 1 (34 sts).

Rnds 9–14 (6 Rnds): Sc in each st (34 sts). Continue to stuff the Head.

Rnd 15: Sc 9, (dec, sc 2) 3 times, sc 5, (dec, sc 2) 2 times (29 sts).

Rnd 16: Dec, sc 27 (28 sts).

Rnd 17: Sc in each st (28 sts).

Rnd 18: Sc 11, (dec, sc) 5 times, dec (22 sts).

Rnd 19: (Dec, sc 3, dec, sc 4) 2 times (18 sts). Finish stuffing the Head.

Rnd 20: (Dec, sc) 6 times (12 sts).

Rnd 21: Dec 6 times (6 sts).

Fasten off and sew the hole closed.

Ears (make 2)

With MC, make a MR, then sc 6 into the MR (6 sts).

Rnd 1: (With MC, inc. With C2, sc 2) 2 times (8 sts).

Rnd 2: (With MC, sc 2. With C2, sc 2) 2 times (8 sts).

Rnd 3: (With C2, inc. With MC, sc 1. With C2, sc 2) 2 times (10 sts).

Rnd 4: (With C2, sc 2. With MC, sc. With C2, sc 2) 2 times (10 sts).

Rnd 5: (With C2, inc, sc. With MC, sc 1. With C2, sc 2) 2 times (12 sts).

Rnd 6: (With C2, inc, sc 2. With MC, sc 1. With C2, sc 2) 2 times (14 sts).

Rnd 7: (With C2, inc, sc 3. With MC, sc 1. With C2, sc 2) 2 times (16 sts).

Fasten off and leave a 12-inch (30.5-cm) tail for sewing.

Assembly

Sew each Ear onto Rnd 12 of the Head, 4 sts apart. Sew the Tail on the back of Rnd 20 of the Body. Sew the Head onto the neck of the Body. If you aren't using safety eyes, embroider a pair of eyes onto Rnd 6 of the Head, 8 sts apart. Finally, embroider a triangle-shaped nose 2 Rnds tall and 3 sts wide at its widest point on the Head.

The Savvy Small Pets

Small pets have such big personalities! As kids, so many of us begged our parents for a hamster or the goldfish we fell in love with at the local pet store. The good news is that these patterns let us cuddle the pet we always dreamed of. And don't worry about the challenge of crocheting tiny details and features, either; they may be small pets, but I've made them jumbo-sized!

Gala the Guinea Pig

Guinea pigs are more social than hamsters, so they make perfect starter pets! Gala's face is different from Henry's (page 131). You can also try making your guinea pig with different fur colors, like brown and gray!

Skill Level

Beginner

Size

Approx 10.5 inches (27 cm) long, 6 inches (15 cm) wide, and 5.25 inches (13.5 cm) tall

Yarn

Super chunky chenille yarn, Premier Yarns Parfait Chunky, 100% polyester, 131 yards (120 m), 3.5 oz (100 g)

- Toffee (MC), 393 yds (360 m)
- Cream (C1), 131 yds (120 m)

Hooks

US size H-8 (5mm)

Notions

Polyester fiberfill

Removable stitch marker used to mark the first stitch of the round (and other indicated stitches within a round)

Tapestry needle

Pair of 6-mm safety eyes (optional)

Gauge

20 sc x 18 rounds = 4 inches (10 cm)

Abbreviations

C1 = color 1

Ch(s) = chain(s)

Dec = decrease (crochet 2 sc together)

Flo = front loop only

Inc = increase (work 2 sc into one stitch)

MC = main color

MR = magic ring

Sc = single crochet

Sc2tog = single crochet 2 stitches together

St(s) = stitch(es)

1
2
3
4

Gala the Guinea Pig Pattern

Legs (make 4)

With C1, make a MR, then sc 8 into the MR (8 sts).

Rnd 1: (Inc, sc) 4 times (12 sts).

Rnds 2–5 (4 Rnds): Sc in each st (12 sts). Do not stuff.

Fold the Leg in half and close the open end by sc2tog across the opening (images 1–4). Fasten off and leave a 12-inch (30.5-cm) tail for sewing.

Ears (make 2)

With C1, make a MR, then sc 6 into the MR (6 sts).

Rnd 1: Inc in each st (12 sts).

Fasten off and leave a 3-inch (7.5-cm) tail. Set aside.

Head and Body

With C1, make a MR, then sc 8 into the MR (8 sts).

Rnd 1: (Inc, sc) 4 times (12 sts).

Rnd 2: (Inc, sc 2) 4 times (16 sts).

Rnd 3: (Inc, sc 3) 4 times (20 sts).

Rnd 4: (With C1, inc in the 1st st, sc 4. With MC, inc in the next st, sc 4) 2 times (24 sts).

Rnd 5: With C1, inc in the 1st st, sc 3, inc in the next st, sc 2. With MC, sc, inc in the next st, sc 3, inc in the next st. With C1, sc 3, inc in the next st, sc 1. With MC, sc 2, inc in the next st, sc 3 (30 sts).

Rnd 6: With MC, (inc, sc 4) 3 times, inc in the next st, sc 2. With C1, sc 2, inc in the next st, sc 2. With MC, sc 2, inc in the next st, sc 4 (36 sts).

Rnd 7: With MC, (inc, sc 5) 3 times, inc in the next st, sc 4. With C1, sc, inc in the next st, sc 3. With MC, sc 2, inc in the next st, sc 5 (42 sts).

Rnd 8: With MC, sc 29. With C1, sc 3. With MC, sc 10 (42 sts). If using, attach safety eyes on this Rnd, 19 sts apart.

Rnds 9–13 (5 Rnds): With MC, sc into each st (42 sts).

Rnd 14: (Dec, sc 5) 6 times (36 sts).

Rnd 15: Sc in each st (36 sts).

Rnd 16: Sc 3. Inc in the next 12 sts in the flo. Sc 21 (48 sts). Stuff the Head.

Rnd 17: With C1, sc 4. With MC, sc 25. With C1, sc 4. With MC, sc 15 (48 sts).

Rnd 18: With C1, sc 6. With MC, sc 22. With C1, sc 20 (48 sts).

Rnds 19–25 (7 Rnds): With C1, sc in each st (48 sts).

Rnds 26–27 (2 Rnds): With C1, sc 40. With MC, sc 8 (48 sts). Start to stuff the Body.

Rnds 28–34 (7 Rnds): With MC, sc in each st (48 sts).

Rnd 35: With MC, sc 43. With C1, sc 5 (48 sts).

Rnd 36: With C1, sc 3. With MC, sc 40. With C1, sc 5 (48 sts). Break MC.

Rnds 37–42 (6 Rnds): Sc in each st (48 sts). Continue to stuff the Body.

Rnd 43: (Dec, sc 6) 6 times (42 sts).

Rnd 44: (Dec, sc 5) 6 times (36 sts).

Rnd 45: (Dec, sc 4) 6 times (30 sts).

Rnd 46: (Dec, sc 3) 6 times (24 sts). Finish stuffing the Body.

Rnd 47: (Dec, sc 2) 6 times (18 sts).

Rnd 48: (Dec, sc) 6 times (12 sts).

Rnd 49: Dec 6 times (6 sts).

Fasten off and sew the hole closed.

Assembly

Sew each Leg on the bottom of the Body, 7 sts apart on Rnds 19 and 36. Sew the Ears onto the front of the Head, 8 sts apart on Rnd 13. Sew a triangle-shaped nose onto Rnds 2-3 of the Head (for embroidery guidance, refer to pages 134 to 135 in Henry the Hamster). If you aren't using safety eyes, embroider a pair of eyes onto Rnd 7 of the Head, 19 sts apart.

Henry the Hamster

Hamsters are introverted and smaller than guinea pigs—but sometimes they look so similar, most people don't notice the difference! Although the patterns for the guinea pig and hamster are the same size in this chapter, I made sure to make Henry the Hamster's face look different from Gala the Guinea Pig (page 127), so you'll quickly be able to tell the difference between the two.

Skill Level

Beginner

Size

Approx 10.5 inches (27 cm) long, 6 inches (15 cm) wide, and 5.25 inches (13.5 cm) tall

Yarn

Super chunky chenille yarn, Premier Yarns Parfait Chunky, 100% polyester, 131 yards (120 m), 3.5 oz (100 g)

- Shell (MC), 393 yds (360 m)
- Cream (C1), 131 yds (120 m)
- Bubblegum (C2), 20 yds (18 m)

Hooks

US size H-8 (5mm)

Notions

Polyester fiberfill

Removable stitch marker used to mark the first stitch of the round (and other indicated stitches within a round)

Tapestry needle

Pair of 6-mm safety eyes (optional)

Gauge

20 sc x 18 rounds = 4 inches (10 cm)

Abbreviations

C1 = color 1

C2 = color 2

Ch(s) = chain(s)

Dec = decrease (crochet 2 sc together)

Flo = front loop only

Inc = increase (work 2 sc into one stitch)

MC = main color

MR = magic ring

Sc = single crochet

Sc2tog = single crochet 2 stitches together

St(s) = stitch(es)

Henry the Hamster Pattern

Legs (make 4)

With C2, make a MR, then sc 8 into the MR (8 sts).

Rnd 1: (Inc, sc) 4 times (12 sts).

Rnds 2–5 (4 Rnds): With MC, sc in each st (12 sts). Do not stuff.

Fold the Leg in half, and sc2tog the Leg closed (see images for this technique on page 128 for Gala the Guinea Pig).

Fasten off and leave a 12-inch (30.5-cm) tail for sewing.

Ears (make 2)

With MC, make a MR, then sc 6 into the MR (6 sts).

Fasten off and leave a 3-inch (7.5-cm) tail. Set aside.

Head and Body

With C1, make a MR, then sc 8 into the MR (8 sts).

Rnd 1: Inc 8 times (16 sts).

Rnd 2: With C1, sc 6. With MC, sc 4. With C1, sc 6 (16 sts).

Rnd 3: With C1, inc, sc 3, inc, sc. With MC, sc 2, inc, sc 2. With C1, sc, inc, sc 3 (20 sts).

Rnd 4: With MC, sc 3. With C1, sc 4. With MC, sc 9. With C1, sc 4 (20 sts).

Rnd 5: With MC, inc, sc 3. With C1, sc, inc, sc. With MC, sc 3, inc, sc 4, inc, sc. With C1, sc 3 (24 sts).

Rnd 6: With MC, (inc, sc 2) 8 times (32 sts).

Rnd 7: With MC, (inc, sc 3) 8 times (40 sts).

Rnds 8–16 (9 Rnds): With MC, sc in each st (40 sts). If using, attach safety eyes on Rnd 9, 19 sts apart. Stuff the Head.

Rnd 17: With MC, (dec, sc 3) 8 times (32 sts).

Rnd 18: With MC, sc 4. With C1, inc 8 times in the flo. With MC, sc 20 (40 sts).

Rnd 19: With MC, inc, sc 3. With C1, sc, (inc, sc 4) 7 times (48 sts).

Rnd 20: With C1, sc in each st (48 sts). Start to stuff the Body.

Rnd 21: With C1, sc 32. With MC, sc 16 (48 sts).

Rnd 22: With MC, sc 3. With C1, sc 30. With MC, sc 15 (48 sts). Break C1.

Rnds 23–42 (20 Rnds): With MC, sc in each st (48 sts). Continue to stuff the Body.

Rnd 43: (Dec, sc 6) 6 times (42 sts).

Rnd 44: (Dec, sc 5) 6 times (36 sts).

Rnd 45: (Dec, sc 4) 6 times (30 sts).

Rnd 46: (Dec, sc 3) 6 times (24 sts). Finish stuffing the Body.

Rnd 47: (Dec, sc 2) 6 times (18 sts).

Rnd 48: (Dec, sc) 6 times (12 sts).

Rnd 49: Dec 6 times (6 sts).

Fasten off and sew the hole closed.

Assembly

Sew each Leg on the bottom of the Body, 7 sts apart on Rnds 19 and 36. Sew the Ears onto the front of the Head, 9 sts apart on Rnd 13. Sew a triangle-shaped nose on Rnds 2-3 on the Head (images 1–4). If you aren't using safety eyes, embroider a pair of eyes onto Rnd 7 of the Head, 19 sts apart.

1
2
3
4

Remy the Rabbit

Rabbits can be challenging to care for, but they make such affectionate pets! This is a fun project to work on. You'll want to attach the back legs carefully—so grab your sewing needle!

Skill Level

Intermediate

Size

Approx 6 inches (15 cm) long, 7 inches (18 cm) wide, and 10 inches (25.5 cm) tall

Yarn

Super chunky chenille yarn, Premier Yarns Parfait Chunky, 100% polyester, 131 yards (120 m), 3.5 oz (100 g)

- Toffee (MC), 393 yds (360 m)
- A scrap amount in Pink (C1)

Hooks

US size H-8 (5mm)

Notions

Polyester fiberfill

Removable stitch marker used to mark the first stitch of the round (and other indicated stitches within a round)

Tapestry needle

Pair of 6-mm safety eyes (optional)

Gauge

20 sc x 18 rounds = 4 inches (10 cm)

Abbreviations

C1 = color 1

Ch(s) = chain(s)

Dec = decrease (crochet 2 sc together)

Flo = front loop only

Inc = increase (work 2 sc into one stitch

MC = main color

MR = magic ring

Sc = single crochet

Sl st = slip stitch

St(s) = stitch(es)

Remy the Rabbit Pattern

Tail

With MC, make a MR, then sc 8 into the MR (8 sts).

Rnds 1–3 (3 Rnds): Sc in each st (8 sts).

Fasten off and leave a 12-inch (30.5-cm) tail for sewing.

Front Legs (make 2)

With MC, make a MR, then sc 8 into the MR (8 sts).

Rnd 1: Inc in each st (16 sts).

Rnds 2–3 (2 Rnds): Sc in each st (16 sts).

Rnd 4: Sc 4, dec 6 times (10 sts).

Rnds 5–7 (3 Rnds): Sc in each st (10 sts).

Sl st into the 1st st of Rnd 7. Do not stuff.

Fasten off and leave a 3-inch (7.5-cm) tail. Set aside.

Back Legs (make 2)

Repeat Rnds 1–4 of the Front Leg. Stuff the Leg before you continue. (Only Rnds 1–4 will be stuffed.)

Rnd 5: Sc 5. In the flo, inc 5 times (15 sts).

Rnd 6: In the flo, inc 2. In both loops, sc 13 (17 sts).

Rnds 7–10 (4 Rnds): Sc in each st (17 sts). Finish stuffing Rnds 1–7 before continuing on to the next round.

Rnd 11: Dec 8, sc in last st (9 sts).

Fasten off and leave a 12-inch (30.5-cm) tail. Sew the hole closed. Set aside.

Body

With MC, make a MR, then sc 8 into the MR (8 sts).

Rnd 1: Inc in each st (16 sts).

Rnd 2: (Inc, sc) 8 times (24 sts).

Rnd 3: (Inc, sc 2) 8 times (32 sts).

Rnd 4: (Inc, sc 3) 8 times (40 sts).

Rnd 5: (Inc, sc 4) 8 times (48 sts).

Rnd 6: (Inc, sc 5) 8 times (56 sts).

Rnds 7–10 (4 Rnds): Sc in each st (56 sts).

Rnd 11: Sc 24, (dec, sc 2) 8 times (48 sts).

Rnd 12: Sc 8. Attach a Front Leg by placing your hook into the 5th st of the Leg and the next st of the Body. Sc the sts together. Sc the 4th st of the Leg and the next st of the Body. Sc the 3rd st of the Leg and the next st of the Body together. Sc 2. Attach the second Front Leg the same way as the previous Leg. Sc 32 (48 sts).

Rnd 13: Sc into the next 8 sts of the Body. Sc into the remaining 7 sts of the Leg. Sc into the next 2 sts of the Body. Sc into the remaining 7 sts of the Leg. Sc into the remaining 32 sts of the Body (56 sts).

Rnds 14–15 (2 Rnds): Sc in each st (56 sts). Stuff the Legs.

Rnd 16: Sc 29, (dec, sc 3) 5 times, dec in last 2 sts (50 sts).

Rnd 17: Sc 8, dec, sc 15, dec, sc 23 (48 sts).

Rnd 18: Sc 26, (sc 2, dec) 5 times, dec in last 2 sts (42 sts).

Rnd 19: Sc 7, dec, sc 13, dec, sc 18 (40 sts). Start to stuff the Body.

Rnds 20–21 (2 Rnds): Sc in each st (40 sts).

Rnd 22: Sc 23, (sc, dec) 5 times, dec in last 2 sts (34 sts). Continue to stuff the Body.

Rnd 23: Sc 7, dec, sc 12, dec, sc 11 (32 sts).

Rnd 24: Sc in each st (32 sts).

Rnd 25: Sc 22, dec 5 (27 sts).

Rnd 26: Dec 3, sc 21 (24 sts).

Rnds 27–28 (2 Rnds): Sc in each st (24 sts). Finish stuffing the Body.

Fasten off and leave a 12-inch (30.5-cm) tail for sewing.

Head

With MC, make a MR and sc 8 into the MR (8 sts).

Rnd 1: (Inc, sc) 4 times (12 sts).

Rnd 2: (Inc, sc 2) 4 times (16 sts).

Rnd 3: (Inc, sc 3) 4 times (20 sts).

Rnd 4: Sc in each st (20 sts).

Rnd 5: (Inc, sc 4) 4 times (24 sts).

Rnd 6: (Inc, sc 5) 4 times (28 sts).

Rnd 7: (Inc, sc 6) 4 times (32 sts). Attach safety eyes 8 sts apart.

Rnds 8–16 (9 Rnds): Sc in each st (32 sts). Stuff the Head.

Rnd 17: (Dec, sc 2) 8 times (24 sts).

Rnd 18: Sc in each st (24 sts).

Rnd 19: (Dec, sc 2) 6 times (18 sts).

Rnd 20: (Dec, sc) 6 times (12 sts).

Rnd 21: Dec 6 times (6 sts).

Fasten off and sew the hole closed.

Ears (make 2)

With MC, ch 10.

Inc in the 2nd chain from hook, sc in the next 7 chs, and inc 2 times in the last ch. Turn your work clockwise 180 degrees, so that you can work along the opposite side of the chain. Then, sc in the next 7 chs, and inc in the last ch (22 sts).

Rnd 1: Inc 2, sc 7, inc 4, sc 7, inc 2 (30 sts).

Rnd 2: (Inc, sc) 2 times, sc 7, (inc, sc) 4 times, sc 7, (inc, sc) 2 times (38 sts).

Fasten off and leave a 12-inch (30.5-cm) tail for sewing.

Assembly

Sew each Ear onto Rnd 12 of the Head, 6 sts apart. Sew each Back Leg onto Rnd 7 of the Body, next to the side of each Front Leg. Sew the Tail onto the back of Rnd 20 of the Body. Sew the Head onto the neck of the Body. If you aren't using safety eyes, embroider a pair of eyes onto Rnd 7 of the Head, 8 sts apart. Finally, with C1, embroider a triangle-shaped nose on Rnds 2–3 on the Head (for embroidery guidance, refer to pages 134 to 135 in Henry the Hamster).

Finn the Ferret

Say hello to this long and silly furry pet! Ferrets are small creatures, but I made this version to be large enough for you to snuggle in your lap. Make sure to grab a lot of stuffing so you don't run out!

Skill Level

Advanced

Size

Approx 15 inches (38 cm) long, 7 inches (18 cm) wide, and 10 inches (25.5 cm) tall

Yarn

Super chunky chenille yarn, Premier Yarns Parfait Chunky, 100% polyester, 131 yards (120 m), 3.5 oz (100 g)

- Espresso (MC), 393 yds (360 m)
- Shell (C1), 131 yds (120 m)

Hooks

US size H-8 (5mm)

Notions

Polyester fiberfill

Removable stitch marker used to mark the first stitch of the round (and other indicated stitches within a round)

Tapestry needle

Pair of 6 mm safety eyes (optional)

Gauge

20 sc x 18 rounds = 4 inches (10 cm)

Abbreviations

C1 = color 1

Ch(s) = chain(s)

Dec = decrease (crochet 2 sc together)

Flo = front loop only

Inc = increase (work 2 sc into one stitch)

MC = main color

MR = magic ring

Sc = single crochet

Sl st = slip stitch

St(s) = stitch(es)

Finn the Ferret Pattern

Legs (make 4)

With MC, make a MR, then sc 8 into the MR (8 sts).

Rnd 1: Inc in each st (16 sts).

Rnds 2–3 (2 Rnds): Sc in each st (16 sts).

Rnd 4: Sc 4, dec 4, sc 4 (12 sts).

Rnd 5: Sc 4, dec 2, sc 4 (10 sts).

Rnds 6–7 (2 Rnds): Sc in each st (10 sts).

Rnd 8: Sc 5, inc 2, sc 3 (12 sts).

Rnd 9: Sc 3, (inc, sc) 4 times, sc (16 sts).

Rnd 10: Sc in each st (16 sts). Sl st into the first st.

Fasten off and leave a 3-inch (7.5-cm) tail. Set aside.

Body

With C1, ch 19. Inc in the second ch from hook, and sc in the next 16 chs. Inc 2 times in the last ch. Rotate your work clockwise 180 degrees, so that you can work along the opposite side of the chain. Sc into the next 16 sts, and inc in the last st (40 sts).

Rnd 1: Inc 2, sc 16, inc 4, sc 16, inc 2 (48 sts).

Rnd 2: Sc 2. Attach a Leg by placing your hook into the 10th st of the Leg and the next st of the Body. Sc the sts together. Repeat this process with the 9th st of the Leg and the next st of the Body, the 8th st of the Leg and the next st of the Body, and so on until you've crocheted the 5th st of the Leg and the next st of the Body together. Sc into the next 9 sts of the Body. Attach the next Leg the same way as the previous Leg. Sc 3. Attach a third Leg by placing your hook into the 24th st of the Leg and the next st of the Body. Sc the sts together. Repeat this process with the 1st st of the Leg and the next st of the Body, the 2nd st of the Leg and the next st of the Body, and so on until you've crocheted the 5th st of the Leg and the next st of the Body. Sc into the next 9 sts of the Body. Attach the last Leg the same way as the previous Leg. Sc into the remaining st of the Body (48 sts).

Rnd 3: With C1, sc 2. With MC, sc into the 10 remaining sts of the Leg. With C1, sc into the next 9 sts of the Body. With MC, sc into the remaining 10 sts of the Leg. With C1, sc into the next 3 sts of the Body. With MC, sc into the remaining 10 sts of the Leg. With C1, sc 9. With MC, sc into the remaining 10 sts of the Leg. With C1, sc into the remaining st of the Body (64 sts).

Rnd 4: With C1, sc 3. With MC, sc 9. With C1, sc 42. With MC, sc 9. With C1, sc 1 (64 sts).

Rnd 5: With C1, sc 4. With MC, sc 8. With C1, sc 43. With MC, sc 8. With C1, sc 1 (64 sts).

Rnd 6: With C1, sc 5. With MC, sc 7. With C1, sc 44. With MC, sc 7. With C1, sc 1 (64 sts).

Rnd 7: With C1, sc 6. With MC, sc 6. With C1, sc 45. With MC, sc 6. With C1, sc 1 (64 sts).

Rnds 8–13 (6 Rnds): Sc in each st (64 sts). Stuff the Legs.

Rnd 14: Sc 17, (dec, sc 3) 8 times, sc 7 (56 sts).

Rnd 15: Sc in each st (56 sts).

Rnd 16: Sc 17, (dec, sc 2) 8 times, sc 7 (48 sts).

Rnd 17: Sc 36. Place a st marker in the 20th st. Place your hook into the next st of the Body and the st marker st. Sl st the sts together. Repeat this process with the next st of the Body and the 19th st, the next st of the Body and the 18th st, the next st of the Body and the 17th st, the next st of the Body and the 16th st, the next st of the Body and the 15th st, the next st of the Body and the 14th st, and the next st of the Body and the 13th st. Sc into the remaining 3 sts of the Body (39 sts). Remove the st marker. Stuff the Body. For more info on this section, refer to Blake the Boxer on page 49.

Rnd 18: Sc 16 (16 sts).

Rnds 19–20 (2 Rnds): Sc in each st (16 sts).

Fasten off and leave a 12-inch (30.5-cm) tail for sewing.

To finish the Body, with MC, place your hook into the 21st st of Rnd 18. Sc into the same st. With MC, work into the remaining 15 sts by dec 7 times, sc into the last st (9 sts).

Rnd 21: (Dec, sc) 3 times (6 sts).

Fasten off and sew the hole closed.

Head

With C1, ch 4. Inc in the 2nd ch from hook, and sc in the next ch. Work 4 sc in the last ch. Rotate your work clockwise 180 degrees, so that you can work along the opposite side of the chain. Sc in the next ch st, and inc in the last ch st (10 sts).

Rnd 1: Inc 2, sc, inc 4, sc, inc 2 (18 sts).

Rnd 2: Sc in each st (18 sts).

Rnd 3: With MC, sc 3. In flo, inc 5. In both loops, sc 3. With C1, sc 3, inc, sc 3 (24 sts).

Rnd 4: With C1, sc. With MC, (inc, sc 2) 5 times. With C1, sc 3, inc, sc 4 (30 sts).

If using safety eyes, attach them on this Rnd, 10 sts apart.

Rnd 5: With C1, (sc 4, inc) 6 times (36 sts).

Rnds 6–12 (7 Rnds): Sc in each st (36 sts).

Rnd 13: (Dec, sc 4) 6 times (30 sts).

Rnd 14: Sc in each st (30 sts).

Rnd 15: (Dec, sc 3) 6 times (24 sts). Stuff the Head.

Rnd 16: Sc in each st (24 sts).

Rnd 17: (Dec, sc 2) 6 times (18 sts).

Rnd 18: (Dec, sc) 6 times (12 sts).

Rnd 19: Dec 6 times (6 sts).

Fasten off and sew the hole closed.

Ears (make 2)

With C1, make a MR, then sc 8 into the MR (8 sts).

Rnd 1: Inc 8 times (16 sts).

Rnd 2: Sc in each st (16 sts).

Ch 1. Fold the Ear flat, place your hook into the first and last st of the Rnd, and sc the Ear closed.

Fasten off and leave a 12-inch (30.5-cm) tail for sewing.

Tail

With MC, make a MR, then sc 6 into the MR (6 sts).

Rnds 1–3 (3 Rnds): Sc in each st (6 sts).

Rnd 4: (Inc, sc) 3 times (9 sts).

Rnds 5–8 (4 Rnds): Sc in each st (9 sts).

Rnd 9: (Inc, sc 2) 3 times (12 sts).

Rnds 10–19 (10 Rnds): Sc in each st (12 sts). Stuff the Tail.

Fasten off and leave a 12-inch (30.5-cm) tail for sewing.

Assembly

Sew the Tail to the back of the Body, on Rnd 11. Next, sew five dashes 2 Rnds tall on each foot to create claws. On the Head, sew a trapezoid-shaped nose 2 Rnds tall and 4 sts wide. Any color is fine; I used black in my example. Additionally, if you're not using safety eyes, embroider a pair of eyes on Rnd 4 of the Head, 10 sts apart. Sew each Ear curved, from Rnds 10–13 of the Head, 9 sts apart from each other. Finally, sew the Head onto Rnd 20 of the Body.

Gia the Goldfish

Whether your goldfish lived for years or only for a few months, if you had one as a kid, you know that they're amazing pets to cherish. This pattern is a rounder version of the typical goldfish, so it's perfect for snuggling!

Skill Level

Beginner

Size

Approx 10.5 inches (27 cm) long, 6 inches (15 cm) wide, and 5.25 inches (13.5 cm) tall

Yarn

Super chunky chenille yarn, Premier Yarns Parfait Chunky, 100% polyester, 131 yards (120 m), 3.5 oz (100 g)

- Orange, 393 yds (360 m)

Hooks

US size H-8 (5mm)

Notions

Polyester fiberfill

Removable stitch marker used to mark the first stitch of the round (and other indicated stitches within a round)

Tapestry needle

Pair of 6 mm safety eyes (optional)

Gauge

20 sc x 18 rounds = 4 inches (10 cm)

Abbreviations

BL = back loop

Ch(s) = chain(s)

Dec = decrease (crochet 2 sc together)

Flo = front loop only

Inc = increase (work 2 sc into one stitch)

MR = magic ring

Sc = single crochet

St(s) = stitch(es)

Gia the Goldfish Pattern

Eyes (make 2)

Make a MR, then sc 8 into the MR (8 sts).

Rnd 1: Inc in each st (16 sts). Attach a safety eye in the center of the MR.

Rnds 2–3 (2 Rnds): Sc in each st (16 sts). Do not stuff.

Fasten off and leave a 12-inch (30.5-cm) tail for sewing.

Fins (make 2)

Make a MR, then sc 6 into the MR (6 sts).

Rnd 1: Inc in each st (12 sts).

Rnd 2: (Inc, sc 2) 4 times (16 sts).

Rnd 3: (Inc, sc 3) 4 times (20 sts).

Rnds 4–7 (4 Rnds): Sc in each st (20 sts).

Rnd 8: Dec 10 times (10 sts). Do not stuff.

Rnd 9: Sc in each st (10 sts).

Fasten off and leave a 3-inch (7.5-cm) tail. Set aside.

Head, Body, and Tail

Make a MR, then sc 8 into the MR (8 sts).

Rnd 1: Inc 8 times (16 sts).

Rnd 2: Sc in the flo of each st (16 sts). Place a stitch marker into the BL of the 1st st.

Rnds 3–4 (2 Rnds): Sc in each st (16 sts).

Rnd 5: Place your hook into the 1st st of the Rnd. Place your hook into the marked st on Rnd 2. Sc the sts together. Repeat this process with the remaining 15 sts and their corresponding stitches from Rnd 2 (16 sts).

Rnd 6: Inc in each st in the flo (32 sts).

Rnd 7: (Inc, sc 7) 4 times (36 sts).

Rnds 8–14 (7 Rnds): Sc in each st (36 sts).

Rnd 15: (Dec, sc 4) 6 times (30 sts).

Rnd 16: (Inc, sc 4) 6 times in the flo (36 sts).

Rnd 17: (Inc, sc 3) 9 times (45 sts).

Rnd 18: (Inc, sc 14) 3 times (48 sts).

Rnds 19–31 (13 Rnds): Sc in each st (48 sts).

Rnd 32: (Dec, sc 6) 6 times (42 sts).

Rnd 33: Sc in each st (42 sts).

Rnd 34: (Dec, sc 5) 6 times (36 sts).

Rnd 35: Sc in each st (36 sts).

Rnd 36: (Dec, sc 4) 6 times (30 sts). Start to stuff the Body.

Rnd 37: Sc in each st (30 sts).

Rnd 38: (Dec, sc 3) 6 times (24 sts).

Rnd 39: (Dec, sc 2) 6 times (18 sts).

Rnd 40: Sc in each st (18 sts). Continue to stuff the Body.

Rnd 41: Inc 18 times in the flo (36 sts).

Rnds 42–46 (5 Rnds): Sc in each st (36 sts).

Fold the Tail in half and sc the Tail closed. Fasten off and sew the hole closed.

Assembly

Sew each Fin on the bottom of the Body, 19 sts apart on Rnd 30. Sew the Eyes onto the front of the Head on Rnd 9, 18 sts apart. If you aren't using safety eyes, embroider a pair of eyes onto Rnd 1 of the Eyes.

April the Axolotl

Axolotls, or "water dogs," are a fun pink color and a sweet friend to have. These salamanders are obscure pets, but they're so cute that I had to add them to this collection!

Skill Level

Beginner

Size

Approx 10.5 inches (27 cm) long, 6 inches (15 cm) wide, and 5.25 inches (13.5 cm) tall

Yarn

Super chunky chenille yarn, Premier Yarns Parfait Chunky, 100% polyester, 131 yards (120 m), 3.5 oz (100 g)

- Bubblegum (MC), 393 yds (360 m)
- Hibiscus (C1), 131 yds (120 m)

Hooks

US size H-8 (5mm)

Notions

Polyester fiberfill

Removable stitch marker used to mark the first stitch of the round (and other indicated stitches within a round)

Tapestry needle

Pair of 6-mm safety eyes (optional)

Gauge

20 sc x 18 rounds = 4 inches (10 cm)

Abbreviations

C1 = color 1

Ch(s) = chain(s)

Dec = decrease (crochet 2 sc together)

Hdc = half double crochet

Inc = increase (work 2 sc into one stitch)

MC = main color

MR = magic ring

Sc = single crochet

Sl st = slip stitch

St(s) = stitch(es)

April the Axolotl Pattern

Legs (make 4)

With MC, make a MR, then sc 8 into the MR (8 sts).

Rnd 1: (Inc, sc) 4 times (12 sts).

Rnds 2–5 (4 Rnds): Sc in each st (12 sts). Do not stuff.

Fold the Leg in half, and sc the Leg closed. Fasten off and leave a 12-inch (30.5-cm) tail for sewing.

Gills (make 6)

With C1, ch 8. Sl st in the 2nd ch from hook, ch 3, join with sl st back in the same ch. (Sl st into the next ch, ch 3 [image 1], join with sl st back in the same ch [image 2]) 2 times more (image 3).

Fasten off and leave a 3-inch (7.5-cm) tail. Set aside.

Dorsal Fin

With C1, ch 36. Sl st in the 2nd ch from hook. Sc in the next 10 chs, hdc in the next 15 chs, sc in the remaining 10 chs. Fasten off and leave a 12-inch (30.5-cm) tail for sewing. Set aside.

Head and Body

With C1, make a MR, then sc 8 into the MR (8 sts).

Rnd 1: Inc 8 times (16 sts).

Rnd 2: (Sc 4, inc in the next 4 sts) 2 times (24 sts).

Rnd 3: [Sc 4, (inc, sc) 4 times] 2 times (32 sts).

Rnd 4: [Sc 4, (inc, sc 2) 4 times] 2 times (40 sts).

Rnds 5–13 (9 Rnds): With MC, sc in each st (40 sts). If using, attach safety eyes on Rnd 9, 20 sts apart. Stuff the Head.

Rnd 14: (Dec, sc 3) 8 times (32 sts).

Rnds 15–16 (2 Rnds): Sc in each st (32 sts).

Rnd 17: (Inc, sc 3) 8 times (40 sts).

Rnds 18–20 (3 Rnds): Sc in each st (40 sts). Start to stuff the Body.

Rnd 21: (Inc, sc 4) 8 times (48 sts).

Rnds 22–41 (20 Rnds): Sc in each st (48 sts). Continue to stuff the Body.

Rnd 42: (Dec, sc 6) 6 times (42 sts).

Rnds 43–45 (3 Rnds): Sc in each st (42 sts).

Rnd 46: (Dec, sc 5) 6 times (36 sts).

Rnds 47–49 (3 Rnds): Sc in each st (36 sts).

Rnd 50: (Dec, sc 4) 6 times (30 sts).

Rnds 51–54 (4 Rnds): Sc in each st (30 sts).

Rnd 55: (Dec, sc 3) 6 times (24 sts).

Rnds 56–57 (2 Rnds): Sc in each st (24 sts).

Rnd 58: (Dec, sc 2) 6 times (18 sts). Finish stuffing the Body.

Rnds 59–60 (2 Rnds): Sc in each st (18 sts).

Rnd 61: (Dec, sc) 6 times (12 sts).

Rnds 62–63 (2 Rnds): Sc in each st (12 sts).

Fasten off and sew the hole closed.

Assembly

Sew each Leg on the bottom of the Body, 7 sts apart on Rnds 19 and 36. Sew the Gills onto the front of the Head, 1 st apart on Rnd 10. Sew the Dorsal Fin across the middle of the back on the Body. If you aren't using safety eyes, embroider a pair of eyes onto Rnd 9 of the Head, 20 sts apart.

The Reptiles and Birds

Reptiles and birds are such unique pets to have! Not just because they're a less popular choice, but because they are often more obscure. Although these pets are less fluffy, they are such sweet animals to have in your home! In this chapter, I recreated some popular pets from this unpopular pet group. These pets are made with a blank slate, so feel free to add customization to the patterns, like a long tongue for the gecko or a head feather for the parrot!

Gemma the Gecko

Geckos are such cool pets! They are nocturnal animals, so you won't be tucking them in the covers at night. However, with this cuddly project, you just might.

Skill Level

Intermediate

Size

Approx 6 inches (15 cm) long, 7 inches (18 cm) wide, and 10 inches (25.5 cm) tall

Yarn

Super chunky chenille yarn, Premier Yarns Parfait Chunky, 100% polyester, 131 yards (120 m), 3.5 oz (100 g)

- Lime Green (MC), 393 yds (360 m)

Hooks

US size H-8 (5mm)

Notions

Polyester fiberfill

Removable stitch marker used to mark the first stitch of the round (and other indicated stitches within a round)

Tapestry needle

Pair of 6-mm safety eyes (optional)

Gauge

20 sc x 18 rounds = 4 inches (10 cm)

Abbreviations

Ch(s) = chain(s)

Dec = decrease (crochet 2 sc together)

Flo = front loop only

Inc = increase (work 2 sc into one stitch)

MC = main color

MR = magic ring

Sc = single crochet

Sl st = slip stitch

St(s) = stitch(es)

Special Stitches

Puff Stitch (puff st): Yarn over and insert your hook into the next stitch. Yarn over again and pull up a long loop. (Yarn over and insert your hook into the same stitch. Yarn over again and pull up a long loop) 2 more times. Yarn over and pull through all 7 loops on your hook.

Gemma the Gecko Pattern

Head, Body, and Tail

With MC, make a MR and sc 8 into the MR (8 sts).

Rnd 1: (Inc, sc) 4 times (12 sts).

Rnd 2: (Inc, sc 2) 4 times (16 sts).

Rnd 3: (Inc, sc 3) 4 times (20 sts).

Rnd 4: Sc in each st (20 sts).

Rnd 5: (Inc, sc 4) 4 times (24 sts).

Rnd 6: (Inc, sc 5) 4 times (28 sts).

Rnd 7: (Inc, sc 6) 4 times (32 sts). Attach safety eyes 16 sts apart.

Rnds 8–16 (9 Rnds): Sc in each st (32 sts). Stuff the Head and Body.

Rnd 17: (Dec, sc 2) 8 times (24 sts).

Rnd 18: (Dec, sc) 8 times (16 sts).

Rnd 19: Sc in each st (16 sts).

Rnd 20: Inc in each st around, in the flo (32 sts).

Rnds 21–41 (21 Rnds): Sc in each st (32 sts).

Rnd 42: (Dec, sc 2) 8 times (24 sts).

Rnds 43–45 (3 Rnds): Sc in each st (24 sts). Start to stuff the Tail.

Rnd 46: (Dec, sc 2) 6 times (18 sts).

Rnds 47–49 (3 Rnds): Sc in each st (18 sts). Continue to stuff the Tail.

Rnd 50: (Dec, sc) 6 times (12 sts).

Rnds 51–59 (9 Rnds): Sc in each st (12 sts). Finish stuffing the Tail.

Rnd 60: Dec 6 times (6 sts).

Fasten off and sew the hole closed.

Legs (make 4)

With MC, make a MR, then sc 6 into the MR (6 sts).

Rnd 1: Sc, (sc, ch 4, puff st in the 2nd ch from hook. Sl st in the remaining 2 chs) 3 times total, sc 2 (images 1–2) (15 sts).

Rnd 2: Sc in each sc only (do not sc into the chs or puff st that we worked on Rnd 1; those are the gecko's toes) (image 3) (6 sts).

Rnd 3: Sc in each st (6 sts).

Rnds 4–6 (3 Rnds): Dec 1 time, inc 2 times in the flo, dec 1 time (6 sts).

Rnd 7: Inc 6 times (12 sts). Stuff the Legs.

Rnds 8–9 (2 Rnds): Sc in each st (12 sts).

Rnd 10: Dec 6 times (6 sts).

Fasten off and leave a 6-inch (15-cm) tail for sewing. Sew the hole closed.

Assembly

Sew 2 Legs onto Rnd 20 of the Body, 14 sts apart. Sew the remaining 2 Legs onto Rnd 47 of the Body, next to the side of each Front Leg. If you aren't using safety eyes, embroider a pair of eyes onto Rnd 7 of the Head, 18 sts apart.

Wendy the Worm

We've all had a pet worm before! Whether you kept your own pet worm in your backyard or kept it in your house, these worms can be snuggled. In this rendition, I made Wendy green, but feel free to make your own worm salmon colored!

Skill Level

Beginner

Size

Approx 3 inches (7.5 cm) long, 3 inches (7.5 cm) wide, and 14 inches (35.5 cm) tall

Yarn

Super chunky chenille yarn, Premier Yarns Parfait Chunky, 100% polyester, 131 yards (120 m), 3.5 oz (100 g)

- Lime Green (MC), 393 yds (360 m)
- Shell (C1), 131 yds (120 m)

Hooks

US size H-8 (5mm)

Notions

Polyester fiberfill

Removable stitch marker used to mark the first stitch of the round (and other indicated stitches within a round)

Tapestry needle

Pair of 6-mm safety eyes (optional)

Gauge

20 sc x 18 rounds = 4 inches (10 cm)

Abbreviations

C1 = color 1

Ch(s) = chain(s)

Dec = decrease (crochet 2 sc together)

Flo = front loop only

Inc = increase (work 2 sc into one stitch)

MC = main color

MR = magic ring

Sc = single crochet

St(s) = stitch(es)

Wendy the Worm Pattern

Head and Body

With MC, make a MR, then sc 6 into the MR (6 sts).

Rnd 1: Sc in each st (6 sts).

Rnd 2: (Inc, sc) 3 times (9 sts).

Rnd 3: (Inc, sc 2) 3 times (12 sts).

Rnd 4: (Inc, sc 3) 3 times (15 sts).

Rnd 5: (Inc, sc 4) 3 times (18 sts).

Rnd 6: With MC, inc in the 1st st, sc 5, inc in the next st. With C1, sc 5. With MC, inc in the next st, sc 5 (21 sts).

Rnd 7: With MC, inc in the 1st st, sc 6, inc in the next st, sc. With C1, sc 5. With MC, inc in the next st, sc 6 (24 sts).

Rnd 8: With MC, inc in the 1st st, sc 7, inc in the next st, sc 3. With C1, sc 4. With MC, inc in the next st, sc 7 (27 sts).

Rnds 9–10 (2 Rnds): With MC, sc 14. With C1, sc 5. With MC, sc 8 (27 sts).

Rnd 11: With MC, sc 15. With C1, sc 4. With MC, sc 8 (27 sts).

Rnds 12–13 (2 Rnds): With MC, sc 15. With C1, sc 5. With MC, sc 7 (27 sts).

Rnd 14: With MC, sc 16. With C1, sc 4. With MC, sc 7 (27 sts).

Rnds 15–16 (2 Rnds): With MC, sc 16. With C1, sc 5. With MC, sc 6 (27 sts).

Rnd 17: With MC, sc 17. With C1, sc 4. With MC, sc 6 (27 sts). Start to stuff the Body.

Rnds 18–19 (2 Rnds): With MC, sc 17. With C1, sc 5. With MC, sc 5 (27 sts).

Rnd 20: With MC, sc 18. With C1, sc 4. With MC, sc 5 (27 sts).

Rnds 21–22 (2 Rnds): With MC, sc 18. With C1, sc 5. With MC, sc 4 (27 sts).

Rnd 23: With MC, sc 19. With C1, sc 4. With MC, sc 4 (27 sts).

Rnds 24–25 (2 Rnds): With MC, sc 19. With C1, sc 5. With MC, sc 3 (27 sts).

Rnd 26: With MC, sc 20. With C1, sc 4. With MC, sc 3 (27 sts).

Rnds 27–28 (2 Rnds): With MC, sc 20. With C1, sc 5. With MC, sc 2 (27 sts).

Rnd 29: With MC, sc 21. With C1, sc 4. With MC, sc 2 (27 sts).

Rnds 30–31 (2 Rnds): With MC, sc 21. With C1, sc 5. With MC, sc in last st (27 sts).

Rnd 32: With MC, sc 22. With C1, sc 4. With MC, sc in last st (27 sts). Continue to stuff the Body.

Rnds 33–34 (2 Rnds): With MC, sc 22. With C1, sc 5 (27 sts).

Rnds 35–36 (2 Rnds): With MC, sc 23. With C1, sc 4 (27 sts).

Rnd 37: With C1, sc 1. With MC, sc 22. With C1, sc 4 (27 sts).

Rnds 38–39 (2 Rnds): With C1, sc 1. With MC, sc 23. With C1, sc 3 (27 sts).

Rnd 40: With C1, sc 2. With MC, sc 22. With C1, sc 3 (27 sts).

Rnd 41: With C1, sc 2. With MC, sc 23. With C1, sc 2 (27 sts).

Rnd 42: With C1, sc 2. With MC, sc 22. Inc 1 time in the flo. With C1, inc in the last 2 sts (30 sts).

Rnd 43: With C1, inc in the flo, in the next 2 sts. With MC, inc in the next st, sc 21, inc in the next st, sc 1. With C1, (inc, sc) 2 times (36 sts).

Rnd 44: With C1, (inc, sc) 2 times, inc in the next st. With MC, sc 25. With C1, sc 6 (39 sts).

Rnd 45: With C1, sc 8. With MC, sc 26. With C1, sc 5 (39 sts). Continue to stuff the Body

Rnd 46: With C1, sc 8. With MC, sc 27. With C1, sc 4 (39 sts).

Rnd 47: With C1, sc 8. With MC, sc 31 (39 sts). Break C1.

Rnds 48–53 (6 Rnds): With MC, sc in each st (39 sts). Attach safety eyes into Rnd 48, 12 sts apart. Start to stuff the Head.

Rnd 54: (Dec, sc 11) 3 times (36 sts).

Rnd 55: (Dec, sc 4) 6 times (30 sts).

Rnd 56: (Dec, sc 3) 6 times (24 sts). Finish stuffing the Head.

Rnd 57: (Dec, sc 2) 6 times (18 sts).

Rnd 58: (Dec, sc) 6 times (12 sts).

Rnd 59: Dec 6 times (6 sts).

Fasten off and sew the hole closed.

Assembly

If you aren't using safety eyes, embroider a pair of eyes onto Rnd 48 of the Head, 12 sts apart.

Denny the Duck

Ducks are fun pets, especially if you already have a lot of farm animals. Ducks usually gather in groups, so you might want to make a couple more so that your ducks aren't lonely!

Skill Level

Intermediate

Size

Approx 7 inches (18 cm) long, 5 inches (13 cm) wide, and 10 inches (25.5 cm) tall

Yarn

Super chunky chenille yarn, Premier Yarns Parfait Chunky, 100% polyester, 131 yards (120 m), 3.5 oz (100 g)

- Yellow (MC), 393 yds (360 m)
- Orange (C1), 131 yds (120 m)

Hooks

US size H-8 (5mm)

Notions

Polyester fiberfill

Removable stitch marker used to mark the first stitch of the round (and other indicated stitches within a round)

Tapestry needle

Pair of 6-mm safety eyes (optional)

Gauge

20 sc x 18 rounds = 4 inches (10 cm)

Abbreviations

C1 = color 1

Ch(s) = chain(s)

Dec = decrease (crochet 2 sc together)

Flo = front loop only

Inc = increase (work 2 sc into one stitch)

MC = main color

MR = magic ring

Sc = single crochet

Sc2tog = single crochet 2 stitches together

Sl st = slip stitch

St(s) = stitch(es)

Denny the Duck Pattern

Wings (make 2)

With MC, make a MR, then sc 8 into the MR (8 sts).

Rnd 1: Inc in each st (16 sts).

Rnd 2: (Inc, sc) 8 times (24 sts).

Rnds 3–6 (4 Rnds): Sc in each st (24 sts).

Rnd 7: (Dec, sc) 8 times (16 sts).

Rnds 8–10 (3 Rnds): Sc in each st (16 sts).

Rnd 11: (Dec, sc 2) 4 times (12 sts).

Rnd 12: Sc in each st (12 sts).

Rnd 13: (Dec, sc) 4 times (8 sts).

Wings are not stuffed.

Fasten off and leave a 12-inch (30.5-cm) tail for sewing.

Legs (make 2)

With C1, make a MR, then sc 6 into the MR (6 sts).

Rnd 1: Inc in each st (12 sts).

Rnds 2–3 (2 Rnds): Sc in each st (12 sts).

Fold the Leg in half and close the open end by sc2tog across the opening.

Fasten off and leave a 3-inch (7.5-cm) tail. Set aside.

Beak

With C1, make a MR, then sc 8 into the MR (8 sts).

Rnd 1: Sc in each st (8 sts).

Rnd 2: Sc, inc in the next 2 sts, sc 3, inc in the last 2 sts (12 sts).

Rnd 3: Sc, inc in the next 4 sts, sc 3, inc in the last 4 sts (20 sts).

Fasten off and leave a 12-inch (30.5-cm) tail for sewing. Set aside.

Body

With MC, ch 11. Inc in the 2nd chain from hook, sc in the next 8 chs. Inc 2 times in the last ch. Rotate your work clockwise 180 degrees, so that you can work along the opposite side of the chain. Sc in the next 8 chs, and inc in the last ch (24 sts).

Rnd 1: Inc in the next 2 sts, sc 8, inc in the next 4 sts, sc 8, inc in the last 2 sts (32 sts).

Rnd 2: (Inc, sc 3) 8 times (40 sts).

Rnd 3: Sc in each st (40 sts).

Rnd 4: (Inc, sc 4) 8 times (48 sts).

Rnd 5: (Inc, sc 5) 8 times (56 sts).

Rnd 6: (Inc, sc 6) 8 times (64 sts).

Rnd 7–16 (10 Rnds): Sc in each st (64 sts).

Rnd 17: (Dec, sc 6) 8 times (56 sts).

Rnd 18: Sc in each st (56 sts).

Rnd 19: (Dec, sc 5) 8 times (48 sts).

Rnd 20: Sc in each st (48 sts).

Rnd 21: (Dec, sc 4) 8 times (40 sts).

Rnd 22: Sc in each st (40 sts).

Rnd 23: Sc 26. Place a st marker in the 27th and the 28th sts from the beginning of the round. Place your hook into the 1st and 2nd sts (images 1–2). Sl st the sts together (image 3). Repeat this process with the next st of the Body and the 26th st, the next st of the Body and the 25th st, the next st of the Body and the 24th st, the next st of the Body and the 23rd st, the next st of the Body and the 22nd st, the next st of the Body and the 21st st, the next st of the Body and the 20th st, and the next st of the Body and the 19th st (image 4). Sc into the remaining 4 sts of the Body (30 sts). Remove the st markers.

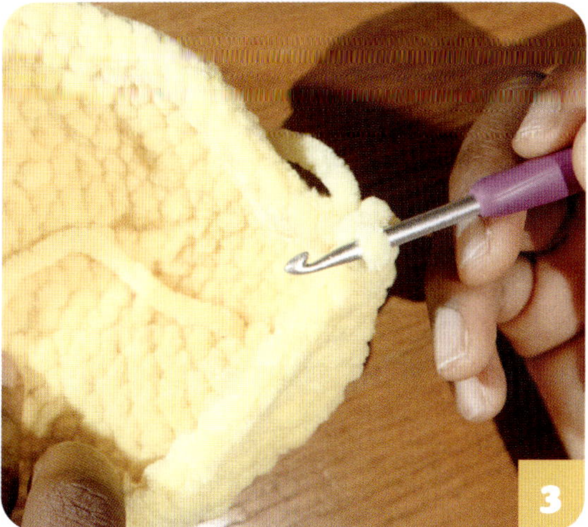

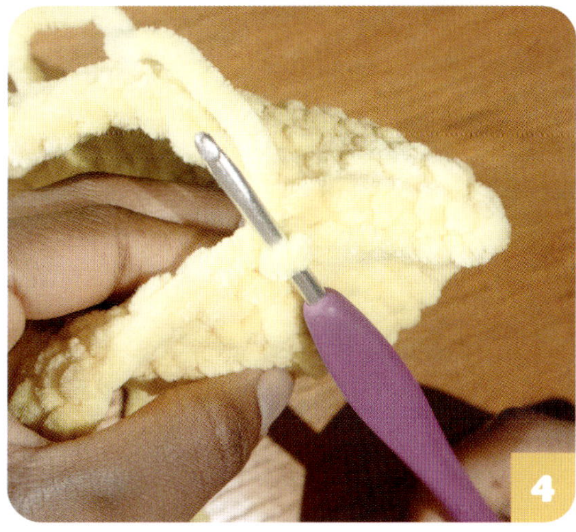

Rnd 24: Sc 22 (22 sts). Stuff the Body.

Rnd 25: Sc in each st (22 sts).

Rnd 26: Sc 3. Inc 10 times in the flo. In both loops, sc 9 (32 sts).

Rnd 27: (Inc, sc 3) 8 times (40 sts).

Rnds 28–37 (10 Rnds): Sc in each st (40 sts). If using, attach safety eyes on Rnd 31, 10 sts apart.

Rnd 38: (Dec, sc 3) 8 times (32 sts). Stuff the Head.

Rnd 39: (Dec, sc 2) 8 times (24 sts).

Rnd 40: (Dec, sc) 8 times (16 sts).

Rnd 41: Dec 8 times (8 sts).

Fasten off and sew the hole closed.

Assembly

Sew each Wing onto each side of the Body. Sew each Leg on the bottom of the Body, 7 sts apart. Sew the Beak onto the front of the Head, between Rnds 26–30 of the Body. Sew the Head onto the neck of the Body. Finally, if you aren't using safety eyes, embroider a pair of eyes onto Rnd 31 of the Head, 10 sts apart.

Perry the Parrot

Although hard to take care of, parrots are one of the most intelligent birds! This version is a bigger-than-life rendition, so you'll need more yarn than the other projects in this book require. Feel free to crochet your own feathers to add to your parrot for personality!

Skill Level

Beginner

Size

Approx 6 inches (15 cm) long, 7 inches (18 cm) wide, and 16 inches (40.5 cm) tall

Yarn

Super chunky chenille yarn, Premier Yarns Parfait Chunky, 100% polyester, 131 yards (120 m), 3.5 oz (100 g)

- Lime Green (MC), 393 yds (360 m)
- Yellow (C1), 131 yds (120 m)
- Red (C2), 131 yds (120 m)

Hooks

US size H-8 (5mm)

Notions

Polyester fiberfill

Removable stitch marker used to mark the first stitch of the round (and other indicated stitches within a round)

Tapestry needle

Pair of 6 mm safety eyes (optional)

Gauge

20 sc x 18 rounds = 4 inches (10 cm)

Abbreviations

C1 = color 1

C2 = color 2

Ch(s) = chain(s)

Dec = decrease (crochet 2 sc together)

Flo = front loop only

Inc = increase (work 2 sc into one stitch)

MC = main color

MR = magic ring

Sc = single crochet

Sl st = slip stitch

St(s) = stitch(es)

Perry the Parrot Pattern

Legs (make 2)

With C1, make a MR, then sc 8 into the MR (8 sts).

Rnd 1: Inc in each st (16 sts).

Rnds 2–3 (2 Rnds): Sc in each st (16 sts).

Rnd 4: Sc 4, dec 6 times (10 sts).

Rnds 5–7 (3 Rnds): Sc in each st (10 sts).

Sl st into the 1st st of Rnd 7.

Fasten off and leave a 3-inch (7.5-cm) tail. Set aside.

Wings (make 2)

Note: The wings are not stuffed.

With C1, make a MR, and sc 8 into the MR. Alternatively, ch 2 and sc 8 into the 2nd ch from hook (8 sts).

Rnd 1: Sc in each st (8 sts).

Rnd 2: (Inc, sc) 4 times (12 sts).

Rnds 3–6 (4 Rnds): Sc in each st (12 sts).

Rnd 7: (Inc, sc 2) 4 times (16 sts).

Rnd 8: Sc in each st (16 sts).

Rnd 9: (Inc, sc 3) 4 times (20 sts).

Rnds 10–13 (4 Rnds): With C1, sc in each st (20 sts).

Rnd 14: (Inc, sc 4) 4 times (24 sts). Break C1.

Rnd 15: With MC, (inc, sc 3) 6 times (30 sts).

Rnd 16: (Inc, sc 4) 6 times (36 sts).

Rnd 17: (Inc, sc 5) 6 times (42 sts).

Rnd 18: (Inc, sc 6) 6 times (48 sts).

Rnds 19–25 (7 Rnds): Sc in each st (48 sts).

Rnd 26: (Dec, sc 6) 6 times (42 sts).

Rnd 27: Sc in each st (42 sts).

Rnd 28: (Dec, sc 5) 6 times (36 sts).

Rnd 29: Sc in each st (36 sts).

Rnd 30: (Dec, sc 4) 6 times (30 sts).

Rnds 31–33 (3 Rnds): Sc in each st (30 sts).

Rnd 34: (Dec, sc 3) 6 times (24 sts).

Rnd 35: Sc in each st (24 sts).

Rnd 36: (Dec, sc 2) 6 times (18 sts).

Rnd 37: Sc in each st (18 sts).

Rnd 38: (Dec, sc) 6 times (12 sts).

Rnd 39: Dec 6 times (6 sts).

Fasten off and sew the hole closed. Fold the Wing in half so that it looks like a bowl. Set aside.

Tail, Body, and Head

With C1, make a MR and sc 6 into the MR (6 sts).

Rnd 1: Inc 6 times (12 sts).

Rnds 2–4 (3 Rnds): Sc in each st (12 sts). Break C1.

Rnd 5: With MC, (inc, sc 2) 4 times (16 sts).

Rnds 6–8 (3 Rnds): Sc in each st (16 sts).

Rnd 9: (Inc, sc 3) 4 times (20 sts).

Rnds 10–11 (2 Rnds): Sc in each st (20 sts).

Rnd 12: (Inc, sc 4) 4 times (24 sts).

Rnds 13–15 (3 Rnds): Sc in each st (24 sts).

Rnd 16: (Inc, sc 3) 6 times (30 sts).

Rnd 17: Sc in each st (30 sts).

Rnd 18: Sc 12, (inc, sc 2) 6 times (36 sts).

Rnd 19: Sc 12, (inc, sc 3) 6 times (42 sts).

Rnd 20: (Inc, sc 6) 6 times (48 sts).

Rnd 21: Sc in each st (48 sts).

Rnd 22: (Inc, sc 7) 6 times (54 sts).

Rnds 23–26 (4 Rnds): Sc in each st (54 sts).

Rnd 27: (Dec, sc 2) 6 times, sc 6, (inc, sc 2) 6 times, sc 6 (54 sts).

Rnds 28–35 (8 Rnds): Sc in each st (54 sts).

Rnd 36: (Dec, sc 7) 6 times (48 sts).

Rnd 37: Sc in each st (48 sts). Stuff the Tail and Body.

Rnd 38: (Dec, sc 2) 6 times, sc 24 (42 sts).

Rnd 39: (Dec, sc) 6 times, sc 24 (36 sts).

Rnd 40: With MC, sc 2. With C1, sc 3. With MC, sc. With C1, sc 3. With MC, sc 11. In the flo, inc 6. In both loops, sc 10 (42 sts).

Rnd 41: With MC, sc 2. With C1, sc 18, (inc, sc) 6 times, (dec, sc 3) twice (46 sts). Break MC.

Rnd 42: With C1, (dec, sc 3) 4 times, sc 26 (42 sts).

Rnd 43: Sc 34, (dec, sc 2) 2 times (40 sts).

Rnd 44: (Dec, sc 2) 4 times, sc 24 (36 sts).

Rnd 45: Sc 30, (dec, sc) twice (34 sts).

Rnd 46: (Dec, sc) 4 times, sc 22 (30 sts).

Rnd 47: Sc 26, dec 2 (28 sts). Stuff the Body.

Rnd 48: Dec 4, sc 14, (dec, sc) twice (22 sts).

Rnd 49: (Dec, sc) 4 times, sc 10 (18 sts).

Rnd 50: Sc 16. In the flo, inc 2 (20 sts).

Rnd 51: In the flo, inc 4. In both loops, sc 12, (inc, sc) 2 times (26 sts).

Rnd 52: (Inc, sc) 4 times, sc 18 (30 sts).

Rnds 53–57 (5 Rnds): Sc in each st (30 sts). Attach safety eyes on Rnd 53, 9 sts apart.

Rnd 58: (Dec, sc 3) 6 times (24 sts). Stuff the Head.

Rnd 59: (Dec, sc 2) 6 times (18 sts).

Rnd 60: (Dec, sc) 6 times (12 sts).

Rnd 61: Dec 6 times (6 sts).

Fasten off and sew the hole closed.

Beak

With C1, make a MR, and sc 4 into the MR.

Rnd 1: Inc 4 times (8 sts).

Rnd 2: Sc in each st (8 sts).

Rnd 3: Sc 2. In the flo, inc 3. In both loops, sc 3 (11 sts).

Rnd 4: Sc in each st (11 sts).

Rnd 5: With C1, sc 3. With C2, sc 6. With C1, sc 2 (11 sts).

Fasten off and leave a 6-inch (15-cm) tail for sewing.

Assembly

Sew the Beak onto Rnd 54 of the Head. Sew each Wing on the side of the Body, lying flat. If you aren't using safety eyes, embroider a pair of eyes onto Rnd 53 of the Head, 9 sts apart.

Acknowledgments

Thank you to my Mom and Dad, for their consistent support and appreciation for my craft—even when I didn't feel as confident. I love you both.

Thank you to Caleb, who supported me in more ways than he realized. I love you.

A huge thank you to the team at Page Street! They have dealt with my many typos, given me grace with due dates, and more. Thank you for giving me this opportunity.

Special thanks to my pattern testers. This book wouldn't be much without your critique.

And last but not least, I thank God for providing me with this incredible opportunity and the mind to be able to see it through.

About the Author

Glory Shofowora, also known on social media as Crafting in Glory, has grown up crocheting and working with every craft medium available. Although she's crocheted a lot of different items, she's been crocheting unique stuffed animals and plushies and sharing her passion since 2021.

In addition to crocheting custom pet orders, she also works a full-time job as a math teacher. When she's not crocheting, she's playing online games with her siblings. You can find her on Instagram and TikTok @craftinginglory or her website craftinginglory.com.

Index

Page numbers in **boldface** indicate images.

A

B

C

D

E

F